The Limits of Defiance:

Strikes, Rights, and Government

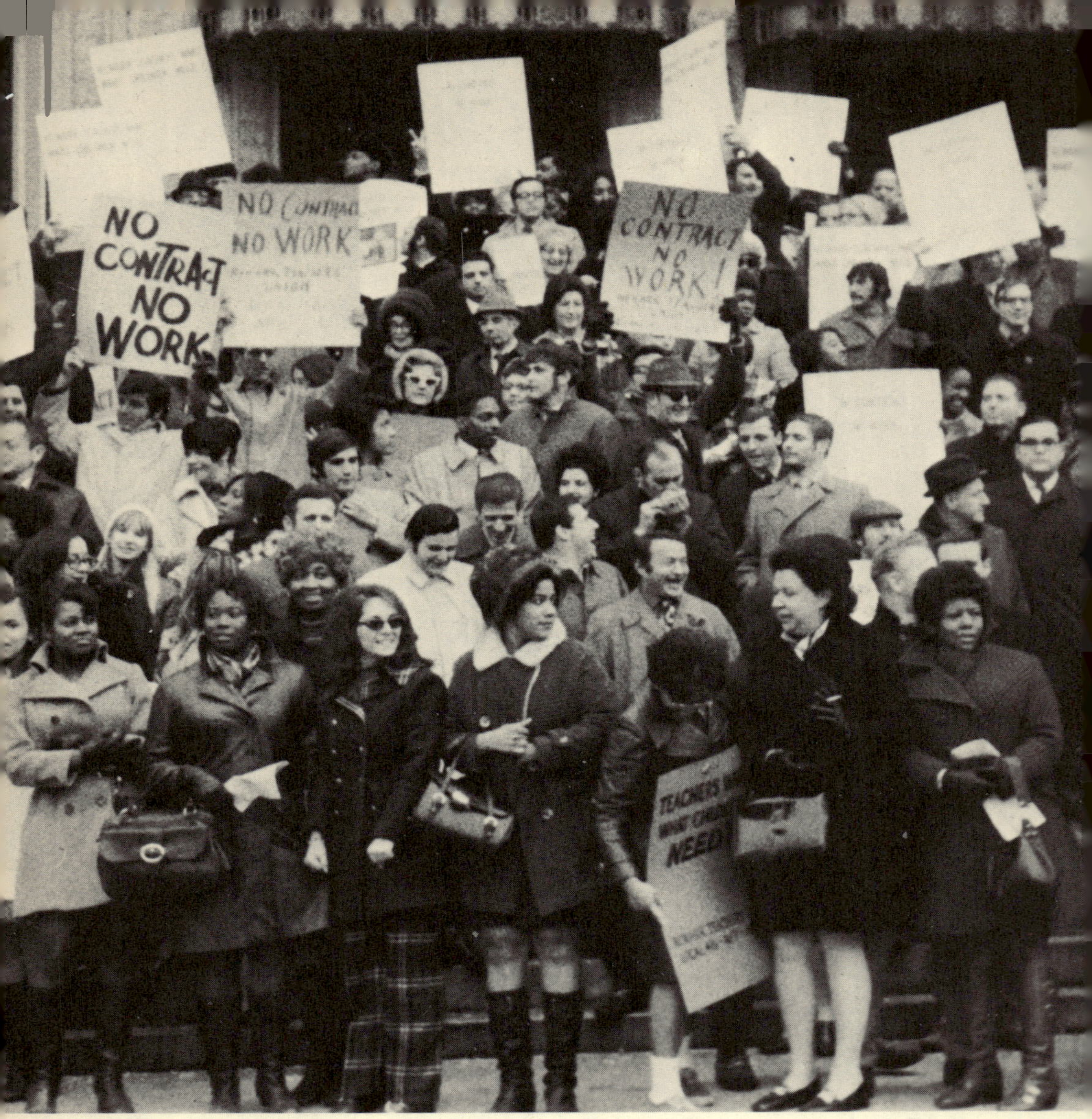
NO CONTRACT NO WORK
NO CONTRACT NO WORK!

The Limits of Defiance:

Strikes, Rights, and Government

by
ROBERT A. LISTON

Franklin Watts, Inc.
845 Third Avenue
New York, N.Y. 10022

The photographs on pages 30 and 107 appear through the courtesy of Culver Pictures, Inc. All other photographs are courtesy of United Press International.

SBN 531–01980–2
Copyright © 1971 by Robert A. Liston
Library of Congress Catalog Card Number: 73–149012
Printed in the United States of America
1 2 3 4 5

To one of these workers
Elinore Cunning
...and in memory of Elden

Contents

		Introduction	ix
Chapter	1	A New and Difficult Problem	3
Chapter	2	Spoils, Reform, and Apathy	20
Chapter	3	A Search for Causes	32
Chapter	4	A Pattern of Neglect	51
Chapter	5	Strikes in Three Cities	67
Chapter	6	Strikes Are Illegal	82
Chapter	7	Are Public and Private Employers the Same?	95
Chapter	8	Can Collective Bargaining Prevent Public Strikes?	105
Chapter	9	The Search for a Better Way	123
Chapter	10	A Look at the Future	138
		Index	146

Garbage piles up in New Orleans during a strike by the city's sanitation workers.

Introduction

A NEW PHENOMENON has burst upon the American scene —strikes by government employees. This book deals exclusively with that problem; in no sense is it a history of either the labor movement or the civil service system.

I have tried to explain why work stoppages by public employees are so serious and why they pose a new and difficult obstacle for Americans. I have tried to examine the causes for the strikes and have dwelt at length upon the various solutions being offered to the problem.

I am indebted to two people who gathered invaluable research materials for me: long-time editor and writer, and my good friend, Clyde F. Newstrand; and Mrs. Eleanor R. Seagraves of Washington, D.C., who performed a small miracle in obtaining information from the labyrinth of Washington bureaucracy, as well as from many private sources.

The Limits of Defiance:

Strikes, Rights, and Government

CHAPTER 1

A New and Difficult Problem

"STRIKE! STRIKE!"

With those words, along with a chorus of hisses and catcalls and the thunder of stamping feet, about two hundred thousand of the nation's more than seven hundred thousand postal employees silenced their union leaders and went on strike against the United States government in March, 1970.

The strike began in New York City and quickly spread to dozens of cities nationwide. Within minutes after the work stoppage began, mail started to pile up by the ton in post offices and warehouses. Business, financial, and governmental affairs became instantly snarled. Continuation of the strike posed a most serious threat to the health and safety of the nation and of individual Americans.

Although the strike lasted only about a week, it served to dramatize in a highly visible way a new and difficult problem facing all Americans—strikes by government employees. A little more than ten years ago, strikes by policemen, firemen, teachers, sanitation men, transit workers,

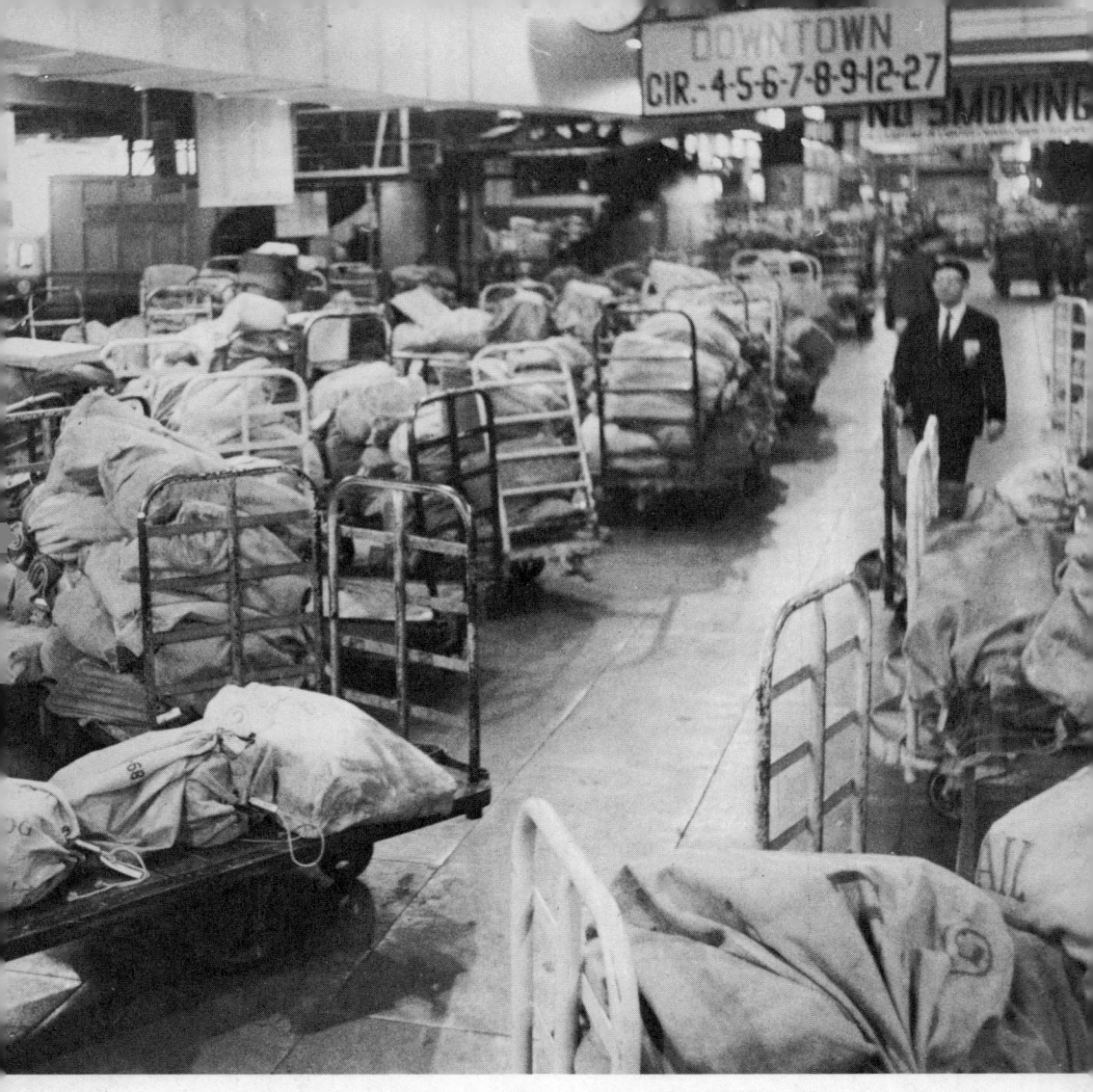

March, 1970, saw the first postal strike in American history and the stoppage of the nation's mail service.

hospital employees, airport controllers, and other types of civil service employees were so rare as to be virtually unnoticed. In 1958, there were only 15 work stoppages by about 2,000 public employees. By 1966, the nation experienced 142 strikes by 105,000 public workers, and the number was growing. In 1968, there were 254 strikes conducted by 202,000 individuals. A year later there were 414 strikes against the government.

By 1970, strikes by public employees reached alarming proportions. Consider the following "strike calendar" prepared by the Labor-Management Relations Service, a relatively new organization sponsored by the United States Conference of Mayors, the National League of Cities, and the National Association of Counties. The calendar, based upon information compiled by the United States Bureau of Labor Statistics, covers the period between January 1 and March 18, 1970. Teachers are not included.

- Jan. 2 Racine, Wisconsin, firemen out 3 days.
- Jan. 5 Middletown, Ohio, sanitation and street repairmen strike 15 days.
- Jan. 6 Cincinnati, Ohio, 1,200 sanitation, highway maintenance, and water department employees out 34 days.
- Jan. 16 Jersey City, New Jersey, sanitation and water department workers walk out.
- Jan. 21 St. Clairsville, Ohio, 25 village employees (police, light, water, street, sewer, etc.) strike.
- Jan. 21 Evansville, Indiana, water department strikes; violence follows.
- Jan. 22 Bexley, Ohio, sanitation and street maintenance men stop work.
- Jan. 26 Bedford, Ohio, 30 service department employees walk out.

Jan. 26 Indianapolis, Indiana, 30 Housing Authority employees out 19 days.

Jan. 27 Ravenna, Ohio, police strike 12 days.

Feb. 2 Reading, Pennsylvania, sanitation truck drivers off job.

Feb. 3 Whitehall, Pennsylvania, 13 highway maintenance men strike for week.

Feb. 5 Charlotte, North Carolina, sanitation strike.

Feb. 7 Toledo, Ohio, 700 police on "sick call" for 2 days.

Feb. 9 Atalla, Alabama, 32 sanitation workers stop work.

Feb. 16 Livonia, Michigan, police force gets the "flu."

Feb. 19 Circleville, Ohio, firemen sick.

Feb. 23 West Milwaukee, Wisconsin, sanitation walkout.

Feb. 24 Los Angeles, California, unit of Department of Social Services strikes.

Feb. 25 Santa Rosa, California, 100 city employees refuse to work.

Feb. 26 Boston, Massachusetts, 120 Boston Housing Authority white-collar workers walk out of 15 housing projects.

Mar. 5 Waterbury, Connecticut, sanitation workers stop work.

Mar. 18 Atlanta, Georgia, 2,600 sanitation workers begin strike.

In the first two and a half months of 1970, there were fifty-one strikes by municipal employees (including teachers)—an average of *one every day and a half.*

As this short strike calendar shows, work stoppages are occurring among public employees all over the country. Every level of government—federal, state, city, county,

A NEW AND DIFFICULT PROBLEM

and township—is being affected. Scarcely an inhabited place, from the largest megalopolis to the smallest hamlet, has failed to feel the pinch of such strikes.

But even the listing of strikes does not truly convey the magnitude of the problem, for there were thousands of threatened strikes that were avoided by last-minute negotiations. Indeed, public employees are organizing and agitating all over the nation. Their unions are the fastest growing in the entire labor movement. In 1956, fewer than 1 million government employees belonged to unions. They accounted for only about 5 percent of all unionized workers. By 1970, more than 2.6 million public workers belonged to unions—and unknown millions more belonged to employee associations, which often act as unions.

The largest such union is the American Federation of State, County, and Municipal Employees, which is abbreviated AFSCME and pronounced af-skē-mē. In 1965 it had approximately two hundred thousand members; by 1970 it had nearly five hundred thousand members, and was still growing at the rate of about one thousand members a month. AFSCME is one of the largest unions in the AFL-CIO (American Federation of Labor-Congress of Industrial Organizations) and is expected to surpass in size such unions as the Teamsters and the United Auto Workers, which have over a million members each.

Union membership alone does not tell the full story. A study by the International City Management Association estimates that some type of government employee organization presently exists in at least seventy-five of the nation's cities. These organizations represent 64 percent of the personnel employed by local government, and they, too, are growing at a fantastic rate. Membership increased by more than 130 percent between 1967 and 1969.

Thus, public workers are organizing, demanding higher

This back-up of jet aircraft waiting for takeoff at Newark Airport in New Jersey is the result of an air controllers' slowdown.

wages and other benefits, and, if necessary, they are either striking or engaging in a variety of "job actions" to enforce their demands. One common form of job action is the "sick-out," during which large numbers of employees claim to be sick and do not report to work. Colorful names, determined by the type of workers involved, have been attached to this form of job action. A sick-out by police is called the "blue flu"; the "red flu" is used for firemen, and the "white flu" for hospital workers.

Another form of job action is the "slowdown"—workers simply dawdle at their tasks or refuse to perform certain services. For example, firemen have refused to engage in fire prevention activities, policemen to write traffic tickets. Working by the "rule book" is still another form of job action, used particularly by air controllers, transit employees, and other transportation workers. By rigidly carrying out a host of dusty regulations, workers can cut service in half.

When any form of work stoppage takes place, the effects upon Americans range from serious to disastrous.

It may be said that all strikes, whether by private or public employees, are serious. Yet, the effects of even a large strike in private industry pale beside those of one by public employees. Realization of this fact begins with the recognition that America is an urban society. Seventy percent of the population lives in or near cities. The urban American lives a most precarious existence in many ways. His is a fragile society utterly dependent upon services provided by employees of public or quasi-public agencies.

There is no shortage of examples. Think of what life in a city would be like without police services. The mere existence of a police force is considered a major deterrent to crime. It is feared that without police protection, criminals, looters, and vandals would run rampant. Of added significance is the work the police do directing traffic and coping with such emergencies as illness or accidents. If policemen were on strike, simply calling an ambulance would be difficult in most cities.

A strike by firemen has always been considered unthinkable. The crowded environment of large cities, many of which contain square mile upon square mile of ancient buildings that are little more than firetraps, makes the danger of death by fire a high risk, even with a functioning fire department. About eight thousand people a year die from fire, and property losses are about $1.5 billion annually, despite the best efforts of firefighters. With these brave men on strike, the risk of an uncontrollable conflagration is staggering, to say the least. For the most part, an urban dweller is totally dependent upon a publicly owned water supply and a municipal sewage system. During a recent strike in Cincinnati, Ohio, large amounts of raw sewage were dumped into the Ohio River. A prolonged strike by sewage workers in England is said to have so polluted that nation's rivers and streams that it will be ten years before they return to their former condition.

Many city dwellers have already discovered the problems that develop without sanitation men. Most cities face a difficult problem at best in collecting and disposing of the mountains of refuse produced by their residents each day. When sanitation men strike, the piles reach monumental proportions in only a few days, producing breeding places for rats, other vermin, and disease.

Public transit is in a poor enough state in the United States when it is functioning normally, but when transit workers, such as bus drivers and subway employees, walk off their jobs, urban dwellers discover that even the poorest public transit system is better than none. The 1966

January 14, 1971—New York policemen, in civilian clothes, begin a job action against the city over a pay dispute.

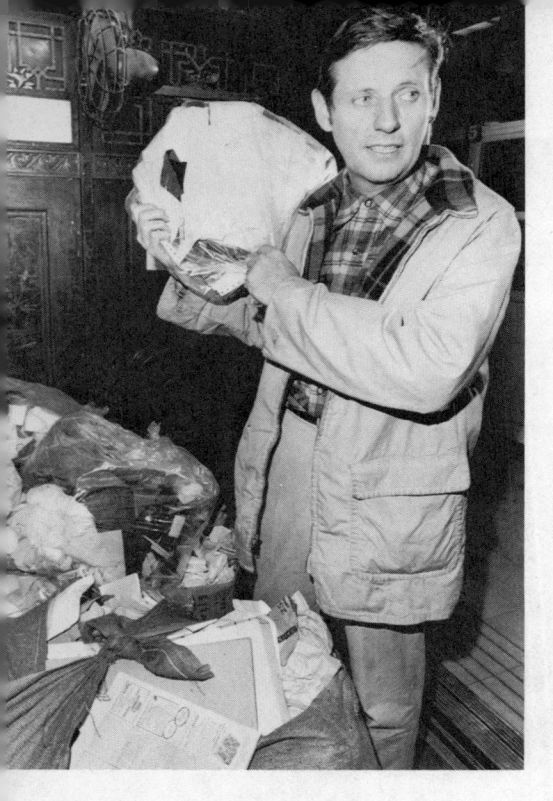

Both in the United States and abroad, city residents have experienced strikes by sanitation workers. Garbage mounts in Pittsburgh (left) and Paris (below).

strike by transit workers in New York City quickly turned that metropolis into one day-long traffic jam. Many wage earners were unable to get to their jobs. Fire engines and ambulances were frequently unable to move through the streets. Truckers had great difficulty delivering food, fuel, and other necessities.

There are also a number of quasi-public agencies that perform services vital to the city dweller. A strike by workers in power plants could cause instant hardship. Consider the 1965 east coast power failure. People were trapped in elevators or subway tunnels. Tens of thousands of people were unable to get home or summon help. The blackout lasted only a few hours, but it was evident that its prolongation would have produced a disaster of major importance. The same results would probably occur if there were a strike.

Similarly, city residents are dependent upon truck and railway workers for delivery of food and fuel, and upon hospital workers to treat the sick and injured.

It is not, however, just the urban dweller who depends upon public employees for essential services. A wintertime strike by highway workers could strand thousands of motorists on snowbound highways, endangering their lives. Even the farmer, who may be temporarily self-sufficient in terms of food, water, and sanitation facilities, needs electrical service and hospital care.

Teachers often contend that the effects of their strikes are minimal. School schedules are flexible, so that the time lost during a short strike can be "made up" by shortening vacation periods. But what would be the effects upon students, particularly high school seniors planning to enter college, if the strike was a long one? A teacher strike can cause other hardships as well—think of the working

With transit workers on strike in 1966, more New Yorkers than ever took to their cars, adding to the city's already heavy traffic.

mothers who are able to take jobs only because their children are safe in school.

No better example of the importance of public employees in American life can be found than in the 1970 postal strike. Americans had always taken the gray-uniformed letter carrier for granted. They were even less aware of the still larger number of postal clerks who sort and dispatch mail inside the post offices. The strike demonstrated the nation's utter dependence upon the postal service, despite the existence of high-speed communications by telephone, telegraph, radio, television, and data processing equipment. Although mail service may be the slowest form of communication, Americans discovered they could not live comfortably without it. Just the week-long strike created chaos that was not straightened out for weeks. If the strike had been prolonged it might have had some of the following effects:

- Much of the nation's financial apparatus, symbolized by the words "Wall Street," would have ground to a halt. Stock exchanges would have been forced to close because purchasers of stock could not be billed and could not make payment to sellers. Banks would have had extreme difficulty billing and collecting on loans and credit accounts.
- Most business enterprises would have been forced to close, for they would have had little chance to bill or collect money. Public utilities, hospitals, railroads, and a host of other enterprises that are dependent upon funds received by mail would have had to shut down.
- The nation's military defense would have been weakened because draft notices could not be mailed to men due for induction into the armed forces. Orders and payments for military supplies would have been inhibited.
- Individuals dependent upon mail-delivered checks would be destitute. Included would be all recipients of

social security, some persons on public welfare, most self-employed people, and retired individuals living on pensions, stock dividends, and bond interest.

- All forms of government would have difficulty collecting taxes. Without a postal service, all government might eventually come to a halt.

Even the lengthy list of vital public and quasi-public employees does not really reach the heart of the matter—the importance of government employees in American life. Government is, by far, the largest employer in the United States. The federal government alone employs nearly 3 million workers, not including members of the armed forces. The sum of the people who work for state and local government dwarfs even that gargantuan figure. Estimates of the number of state and local government employees range from 8.5 to 9.7 *million* people. Every seventh employed person works for some form of government. And the ranks are growing. By 1980, state and local governments are expected to employ 14 million workers.

What do all of these people do? Literally everything. Governments employ just about every occupational specialist from ditch digger to astronaut, nurse's aide to physician, tree trimmer to etymologist, bookbinder to professor. It is in fact a challenge to think of some type of work that a person might do in private employment that does not have its counterpart in government work. Indeed, there are a host of government jobs that have no counterpart in civilian life. Consider only the astronauts and the thousands of specially trained workers who made it possible for them to reach the moon.

Most Americans are unaware of government employees and the tasks they perform. Citizens are aware of the visible workers—the policeman, fireman, letter carrier,

A NEW AND DIFFICULT PROBLEM

teacher, and perhaps a few more—but they seldom come in direct contact with the army of 11 million administrators, scientists, engineers, clerks, and skilled and unskilled workers employed by the federal, state, and local governments.

It is easy to see how government employees permeate the full fabric of American life. Virtually every industry or business experiences some form of government regulation. Public employees inspect meat, fish, and all other foodstuffs, drugs and cosmetics, safety devices on cars, scales, elevators, hospitals, schools, and all structures whether new, old, or under construction. Nothing can be built without a government permit, no sign erected or parade held. Government must be informed when any employee is hired, fired, or retired. Some form of tax is imposed on literally everything—incomes, gasoline, tobacco, amusement, travel tickets, property—the list is endless. More importantly, each year government spending brings hundreds of billions of dollars to defense contractors, farmers, universities, hospitals, schools, transportation companies, book publishers, and manufacturers of literally everything. There seems to be no form of production or service that does not receive money directly or indirectly from the government.

It is relatively easy to imagine what would happen if policemen and firemen were to go on strike. Hundreds of thousands of students can testify to the effects of strikes by teachers. Carry this a bit further. Try to imagine the effects of a strike by the civilian employees of the Defense Department. What would happen to farmers if the employees of the Department of Agriculture struck, to business if the Department of Commerce workers left their jobs, to law enforcement if the Department of Justice were shut down by a strike, to health, education, and welfare if the millions of workers engaged in those fields called a strike for even a brief period of time.

In November, 1968, the American people elected Richard M. Nixon president, and the following January he was sworn into office. Mr. Nixon, a former vice-president, had experience in running the federal government. Within a few weeks of taking office he appointed several hundred people to major government positions, many of whom were inexperienced in government. Certainly they were unfamiliar with their duties and the functions of their subordinates. At best, several weeks elapsed before these high officials came to grips with the problems and tasks confronting them.

The same situation develops each time a new governor, mayor, or other local official is elected, or every time a new official is appointed. Yet, the changeover is hardly observed by the people. No chaos results. Departments and agencies seem to function normally. Why? Because the experienced public workers remain on their jobs during the changeover. They carry on the routine functions of the department, giving the appointed or elected head time to learn his job and to make major policy decisions. This base of permanent civil service workers also explains why officials come and go with little change occurring in the operation of government.

Consider, for just a moment, the chaos that would result if large numbers of public employees went on strike at the moment a new administration was taking office. It has happened on a small scale. In January, 1966, New York transit workers struck just as John V. Lindsay, almost totally inexperienced in municipal affairs, was being sworn in as mayor. The prolongation of the strike was attributable, at least in part, to Mayor Lindsay's unfamiliarity with such problems.

It is no problem to realize that strikes by even a handful of workers can have a most debilitating effect on American life. A work stoppage against the nation's largest corporation is serious, but most Americans can "make do" temporarily if the manufacture of automobiles is halted. However, even short periods without police and fire protection, refuse collection, public transit, highway maintenance, utility operation, postal service, hospital functions —indeed, many other vital governmental activities—can leave citizens helpless. A nation without a functioning government is, by definition, in a state of anarchy.

Five to ten years ago, strikes by public workers were virtually nonexistent. Today hundreds of strikes occur annually. The problem has appeared with breathtaking suddenness. Neither unions nor governments are quite prepared to cope with it, for the problem involves a complex mixture of labor relations, public opinion, politics, race, economic, and taxation matters, and the goodwill or folly of human beings.

Understanding the complexity of labor disputes among public workers must begin with an awareness of what the civil service is and how it got that way.

CHAPTER 2

Spoils, Reform, and Apathy

THROUGHOUT AMERICAN history civil service reform has been one of the great "causes" around which people have rallied. Efforts to improve both the caliber of people working in government and the quality of work they perform have been a consistent theme of reformers since the nation began. Today's agitation and strikes by workers may be interpreted as a continuation of the reform movement.

There has been a lot of reforming to do. To Americans who value honest and efficient government, it is a bit of a shock to learn that there was a time when government jobs were sold to the highest bidder; when people advertised in newspapers, offering to pay for a government job; and when our greatest statesmen were harassed day and night—and even murdered—by job seekers.[1]

When George Washington was inaugurated president, there were about 350 federal employees, mostly clerks.

---

[1] For a fuller account of both the history of the civil service and how it operates read the author's *Your Career in Civil Service* (New York: Julian Messner, 1966).

SPOILS, REFORM, AND APATHY

Washington set out to employ competent men. He specified that an employee must have integrity, experience, education, ability, and general suitability for employment. This was fine, except that most of the people hired were members of Washington's political party, the Federalist Party. John Adams, who succeeded Washington, maintained the same practices as well as many of the same employees.

Thomas Jefferson, the third president, was a member of the Republican (later Democratic-Republican) Party. He was too high-minded to throw out the Federalists, so he waited until he could replace the workers when openings became available through resignation, illness, or death. Before long, Jefferson managed to create a federal service consisting almost entirely of members of his political party.

This situation continued through the terms of James Madison and James Monroe, both Democratic-Republicans. When John Quincy Adams, a Whig, was elected, he refused to disturb the civil service. It was the last time this would happen for a long time.

Andrew Jackson, elected the seventh president in 1828, won the office by attacking what today would be called the "Eastern establishment." He charged that the government was being run by the educated Eastern classes, men of "breeding" and "proper birth," who were out of touch with the "common man," particularly those living in the West, which at that time was the region around the Appalachian Mountains. When Jackson took office he looked at the members of the government and said, "throw the rascals out." That is precisely what he did. Large numbers of government employees were replaced by people who had voted for Jackson.

This wholesale replacement of government workers

when a new president took office became known as the "spoils system." Jackson is wrongly accused of inventing that system, for the principle had been practiced by both Washington and Jefferson. The term was first used in 1832 in New York by United States Senator William Learned Marcy during a debate with Henry Clay of Kentucky over Jackson's nomination of Martin Van Buren as minister to Great Britain. He said, "They see nothing wrong in the rule that to the victor belong the spoils of the enemy."

Clay replied:

> It is a detestable system, drawn from the worst period of the Roman Republic. And if it were to be perpetuated—if the offices, honors and dignities of the people were to be put up to public scramble, to be decided by the result of every Presidential election— our Government and institutions, becoming intolerable, would finally end up in a despotism as inexorable as that at Constantinople.

Few men have been so prophetic as Clay was in this instance. The spoils system ran rampant after 1835, creating a mess of the first magnitude. It may be argued that those days are gone and the practices of the last century are now a mere curiosity. Yet a brief look at the spoils system shows how difficult it was to establish the present system and why it is desirable to maintain this system.

Each change in the presidency has resulted in the replacement of thousands of federal jobholders. Even when a vice-president replaced a deceased president, he reorganized the government. For the first month or two in office, the president did little else but see job seekers. Each had a petition in hand from some local politician stating that he had been faithful to the party, voted correctly, or contributed money.

At one point Abraham Lincoln, who simultaneously faced the problems of the spoils system and the Civil War, said, "I am like a man so busy letting rooms at one end of his house that he has no time left to put out a fire that is blazing and destroying at the other end." On another occasion, seeing a throng of job seekers, he said, "There you see something which will in the course of time become a greater danger to the Republic than the Rebellion itself." While ill with smallpox, Lincoln said to his attendants, "Tell all the office seekers to come in at once, for now I have something I can give to all of them."

The spoils system led to something far worse than the harassment of presidents—dishonesty and inefficiency. The corruption was almost incomprehensible. Advertisements ran in Washington newspapers: "An educated and highly respectable lady desires a position in one of the Government departments; will pay 40 percent of salary for same" or "A reliable gentleman will furnish the best political papers and will pay $150 to anyone who will help him secure a position of any kind in Washington."

It was not uncommon for someone seeking government employment to pay as much as five thousand dollars for a four-year appointment to a job paying a salary of fifteen hundred dollars a year. And even after he bought his job, a worker was not through paying. He was expected to make sizable contributions to the political party in power in hopes of keeping his job after the next election. For years the principal source of campaign funds was the "levy" on officeholders.

Obviously, no one works for nothing. After buying a job and paying to keep it, a government worker compensated himself all too often through graft. To give only one example: At the very start of the spoils system, an audit of the accounts of Samuel Swarthout, Collector of the Port of New York, showed a shortage of $210,000. Nevertheless, he was reappointed to office. During the term of Martin Van Buren, Swarthout fled to Europe with over $1,240,000 in government funds. (One hesitates to think what a million 1840-dollars would be worth today.)

The inefficiency of the spoils system affected America's performance in all its wars, certainly until World War I. In the Mexican and Civil Wars men died for lack of ammunition or because they had inferior weapons, shoddy uniforms and blankets, and wormy, spoiled food purchased by corrupt and unqualified officeholders. In the heyday of the spoils system, men would buy a job, then fill it with someone whom they hired at a lower salary—if the job was filled at all. Considering the abuses, it is amazing that the government operated at all under the spoils system.

Efforts to reform the spoils system went on for decades. In 1853, Congress set a salary scale—$1,250 through $1,800 annually—for four types of clerks in the Washington offices of the Departments of the Treasury, War, Navy, and Interior. Congress also required that applicants take qualifying examinations. But the spoils system quickly brushed aside this reform. The examinations came to consist of such questions as "what did you have for breakfast?"

Still, the demand for reform would not be silenced. It became a "grass roots" issue among the people, and such candidates as Ulysses S. Grant were forced to pay at least lip service to civil service reform. All Grant accomplished, however, was the formation of a commission to study the problem. Rutherford B. Hayes, elected in 1876, was a friend of reform and tried to get legislation through Congress, but failed. Liberal Republican Carl Schurz, who was

Hayes's Secretary of the Interior, managed the first solid accomplishment. He installed a merit system in his department.

Reform got nowhere until July 2, 1881, when President James A. Garfield was setting out on a vacation trip. He was waiting in the old Baltimore and Potomac Railroad Station in Washington when a man pulled a revolver and fired two shots. One bullet cut across the president's arm. The second entered his back. Garfield lingered in misery for two and a half months, then, on September 19, mercifully died.

The assassin, seized after firing the shot, was Charles J. Guiteau. He had written a pamphlet in support of Garfield's candidacy, which, although false and ineffectual, led Guiteau to believe he had swung the election to Garfield. Therefore, he believed himself entitled to an appointment as United States Consul in Paris. When Garfield refused, Guiteau shot him.

This story came out at Guiteau's trial. He was found guilty and was executed on June 30, 1882. But the nation realized it was the spoils system that had actually murdered the president. The demand for reform increased, but again Congress refused to act. It was only after several antireform congressmen were defeated in the election of 1882 that Congress took action. A bill sponsored by Senator George H. Pendleton of Ohio calling for the establishment of the United States Civil Service Commission was passed and was signed into law by President Chester A. Arthur on January 16, 1883.

Civil service reform was a timid, tenuous thing at first, with only a minority of positions covered. Reform received its biggest boost from Theodore Roosevelt, whom President Benjamin Harrison appointed to the Civil Service Commission in 1889. Roosevelt brought his usual vigor to the job of enforcing the federal law. One of his accomplishments was the elimination of the illegal spoils system from the civil service. He personally investigated charges that merit employees were being assessed for political contributions. He is credited with barring assessments from the 1892 election. He also made the system of granting appointments more workable. Roosevelt insisted that qualification examinations be practical and applicable to the actual duties to be performed. Through the use of publicity, he attracted applicants from all over the country, rather than just those living in the Washington area.

Roosevelt resigned in 1895 to become president of the New York City Board of Police Commissioners. In cleaning up the corruption-ridden police department, he introduced competitive examinations for policemen. Later, as governor of New York, Roosevelt strengthened the merit system in that state. Finally, as president he greatly extended the civil service. When he took office only 46 percent of the service was competitive. When he left the White House, 66 percent of the 116,000 positions were classified under the merit system.

This century has witnessed repeated efforts to improve and modernize the civil service. The Retirement Act, which set up a pension system for federal employees, was passed in 1920. In 1923, Congress enacted the Classification Act, which established the principle of equal pay for equal work. The following year, the State Department's Diplomatic and Consular Service was organized into the Foreign Service.

The Great Depression of the 1930's posed a major challenge to the merit system. Presidents Herbert Hoover and Franklin D. Roosevelt both took economy measures—salaries were cut and vacations trimmed. There was even a rule passed stating that wives could not be employed by the government if their husbands worked. The biggest threat came from the resurgence of the spoils system. As Congress created many of Roosevelt's New Deal agencies, they were placed outside the civil service. By 1936, a staggering 325,534 positions, or about 40 percent of the government work force, were outside the merit system. The Civil Service Commission, understaffed and working with reduced appropriations, was inundated with applications from hundreds of thousands of job seekers.

In 1938, President Roosevelt issued two executive orders that had immediate and permanent effects upon the civil service. One stated that all positions that were not exempted by law were in the competitive service. The second established divisions of personnel in the executive departments and agencies. Previously, the Civil Service Commission had existed primarily as a central examining agency. Under the new system, it delegated its responsibilities for examinations to the agency personnel staffs with the understanding that their conduct and operations conform to Commission standards. The Commission thus became a personnel authority, setting rules and developing practices to govern training, placement, promotion, transfers, grievance procedures, and employee relations. The result was more modern personnel management in the federal government.

The system worked in essentially this manner through World War II and the Korean War. In 1962, President John F. Kennedy instituted the most recent reforms. At his urging, Congress passed the Federal Salary Reform Act, which established the principle that federal pay should be comparable to that in private enterprise for work of similar nature. The act calls upon Congress to increase salaries annually to make the pay of government workers approximately equal to that in private industry.

THE LIMITS OF DEFIANCE

At the same time, the Civil Service Commission embraced other reforms. Salaries were to be based upon skill and education rather than the officeholder's title. Thus, a scientist working alone in a laboratory might earn a salary equal to a division chief supervising hundreds of persons. A policy of unlimited transfers was adopted. Any employee who disliked his job or his boss or who felt stymied in seeking a promotion could apply for and accept a job in any other federal agency, while keeping his pension and seniority intact. He would not need the permission of his supervisor to accept the better job.

The changes in pay scales and personnel practices were made in recognition of the changing nature of the federal service. The technological age increased the need for scientists, engineers, doctors, and lawyers, as well as other professional workers, computer programmers, a wide variety of technicians, and highly skilled workers, such as stenographers and aircraft mechanics. Indeed, the federal government employs more professionals in the physical sciences than general clerks, more engineers than typists, more individuals in research and development than in mail and file operations. In a recent year, the federal service included more than 71,000 scientists, more than 116,000 engineers, and more than 78,000 technicians to support the scientists and engineers.

To attract such personnel, the federal government has had to pay salaries that are competitive with private industry—as high as $35,000 a year. The government has had to give these people a sense of accomplishment, responsibility, and maximum opportunity for personal and professional advancement. The federal government has been so successful in its recruiting practices that private industry is hard-pressed to compete, and businessmen have complained about high government salaries.

SPOILS, REFORM, AND APATHY

Civil service reform has been a huge success. The United States has gone from the corrupt and inefficient spoils system to a highly professional civil service at all levels of government. For decades, this system has operated with a minimum of scandal and a maximum of efficiency. The numbers of government employees have increased tenfold and more.

Perhaps it was the very success of civil service reform that led to what one labor leader has called "benign neglect" of government workers. The system worked so well that most Americans thought—if they thought about public employees at all—that it was a blessing to have a trouble-free situation in a world so full of international and national problems.

Many Americans, particularly older ones, had an image of the public employee that, if it was ever true, is as extinct today as the passenger pigeon. Public workers were viewed as part of an "army of clerks in green eyeshades," not very intelligent, not very able, not very adventuresome, dedicated to routine, safety, and security. The best men, it was thought, entered business or the professions. Public employees were people who either could not "make it" on the "outside" or who were afraid to try.

The origins of this notion lay in the spoils system and in America's long-lived enchantment with the Horatio Alger, or rags-to-riches, theme. A poor boy, even an immigrant, could become rich and powerful if he worked hard, saved his money, and applied his native sense to mercantile enterprises. Such giants of industry as Andrew Carnegie and John D. Rockefeller had done it. Had not Lincoln, who was born in a log cabin, become president?

There just had to be something suspicious, vaguely "wrong," and decidedly inferior about a man who chose a career as a green-eyeshaded clerk in a government office

A streetcar workers' strike in 1916 was one of the first job actions by municipal employees.

A 1919 strike by Boston policemen was ended when Governor Calvin Coolidge called in troops.

rather than entering the hurly-burly, winner-take-all world of industry and politics.

Another general public attitude was expressed in the phrase "civil servants," as public employees were frequently called. While no one thought of public workers as slaves, there was a comforting image of these employees as loyal servants obedient to the wishes of the citizens who employed them. Few politicians failed to praise the loyal and faithful civil servants.

The servant image made it unthinkable for public employees to strike. A servant does not rise and smite his master. If he does not like his job, he quits. Someone else is hired who will appreciate the security, retirement plan, and other benefits offered by a generous employer. Besides, it was against the law for public employees to strike. Calvin Coolidge had settled the issue in 1919, when, as governor of Massachusetts, he sent in troops to smash a strike by Boston policemen.

It is only natural, however, that civil servants have complaints. That they want periodic raises in pay—all servants want that. But these were matters to be handled by civil service commissions and politicians. Indeed, weren't pay raises voted? There was no need for citizens to concern themselves.

Then, about 1965, this bubble of apathy burst. Americans were stunned by a series of strikes by transit workers, sanitation men, social workers, and teachers. Policemen, firemen, and a host of other workers agitated and protested, issued demands, threatened strikes, and began a variety of job actions. What had happened? What did these people want?

CHAPTER 3

A Search for Causes

THE WORKINGS OF the civil service system itself are a cause of labor unrest among government employees.

As we have seen, a major element of civil service reform was the classification system, which promised equal pay for equal work. There would be no favoritism. A typist, welder, or engineer was paid the same as another typist, welder, or engineer doing similar work. Classification also ensured that an employee would receive regular salary increases. There are distinct advantages to the classification system and no labor leader even remotely considers doing away with it. But as a practical matter, classification poses difficulties that are at the root of the unrest among government employees.

How does classification work? The federal government has several classification systems. For example, there is one for postal workers, another for blue-collar workers. The biggest system is the General Schedule, abbreviated GS. It is comprised of eighteen classifications—GS-1 to GS-18.

A SEARCH FOR CAUSES

A GS-1 might be a messenger or laboratory aide. A GS-18 might be a division chief with hundreds of individuals working under him. Every job has a classification. A medical aide would be GS-2, a typist GS-3, a hospital clerk GS-4, an administrative assistant GS-5, an engineer GS-7 or GS-9, a physicist with advanced degrees GS-11. Each classification bears a pay scale. All the workers in any classification regularly receive increases in salary until a maximum is reached. For example, if a GS-6 started at $7,294, he would receive increases in pay until he earned $9,481—but this would take him eighteen years.

The only other way to receive a higher salary is through promotion to a higher classification, which occurs frequently. A stenographer beginning at GS-3 may be promoted to secretary (GS-5) and perhaps to administrative assistant (GS-6 or even GS-7). An engineer typically is promoted from GS-7 or GS-9 to GS-11 or higher. It would not be uncommon for him to become a GS-15.

The classification system thus has the advantages of ensuring uniformity and fairness of pay, while maintaining flexibility in terms of advancement and promotion.

There are disadvantages to the system, however. There is almost no provision for rewarding merit. A typist who is particularly able will receive the same salary as another typist who is marginal in his or her abilities. The only incentive to superior work is the opportunity to be promoted to a higher classification.

In many agencies and departments of the federal government the opportunities for promotion are slim. The Post Office is an excellent example. The very nature of the task of delivering the mail requires a large number of postal clerks, letter carriers, and mail handlers. Promotions to supervisor, inspector, or postmaster are rare among the more than seven hundred thousand postal employees.

During the 1970 postal strike, clerks who had formerly stayed behind the scenes joined letter carriers on the picket line.

Thus 90 percent of the postal employees are in the five lowest classifications. At the time of the strike in March, 1970, most postal workers started at a salary of $6,176 a year and rose to $8,442 after twenty-one years of service.

Other agencies, such as the Social Security Administration, Veterans Administration, and General Services Administration, employ large numbers of workers in the lower classifications. The Social Security Administration, which accumulates mountains of data concerning the weekly and monthly payroll deductions of workers and writes and mails millions of checks monthly, employs large numbers of key-punch operators. The chances of a particular operator being selected for promotion are slight.

Most of the unrest among federal employees occurs among workers in the lower classifications. Their work is routine and often not very challenging or satisfying. Their opportunities for advancement are slim. Most of all, they feel their pay scale is too low to permit them to afford the life-style of better-paid Americans. In order to pay for even the necessities of life, many federal workers in the lower classifications have had to "moonlight," that is, take a second job, or have their wives work.

Conversely, there has been relatively little unrest among the workers in the higher classifications. They enjoy more stimulating work, opportunities for advancement, and higher salaries. In the last ten years, the salaries of people in the higher classifications have been raised 80 percent as part of the effort to recruit scientific and professional personnel. In contrast, the earnings of workers in the lower grades increased only 55 percent during the same period.

A similar situation exists among the 9 million or so individuals employed in state and local civil services nationwide. Although these governments employ large numbers of skilled and professional people, their percentage of skilled workers is considerably lower than in the federal government. The great bulk of state and local employees are teachers, policemen, firemen, sanitation workers, transit workers, street and highway employees, and clerical workers.

The simple nature of state and, particularly, local civil services is that there are large numbers of people employed in the lower grades. The types of workers employed by a government are determined by the services for which that government is responsible. A study of the New York City civil service, the nation's second largest, showed that there are *not* more engineers than clerks, as in the federal service. At the time of the study, New York City paid its workers in the lower classifications higher wages than did the federal government, while its salaries for engineers, for example, lagged considerably behind. This reflects the fact that the city of New York had greater need for clerks than for engineers.

New York City also had nothing remotely resembling the federal government's system of unlimited transfers for people in search of personal advancement. No employee could transfer without permission of his immediate supervisor, a policy frequently leaving the ambitious public employee stymied in a "dead-end" job.

There are, however, opportunities for promotion in a municipal service. In the police department, for example, a patrolman can be promoted on the basis of qualifying examinations to sergeant, lieutenant, captain, inspector, and so on. He can rise from foot patrolman to work in a patrol car or as a detective or in a host of other jobs that do not require him to "pound a beat." Fire departments have similar promotions. But, obviously, there are more patrolmen and firefighters than police and fire officers. The simple nature of the work of the sanitation department guarantees that there is far greater need for men to collect refuse than for supervisors; and in the transit department, for more men to operate buses and subway trains than for men to oversee their work.

It is no accident that, as in federal service, many strikes have occurred among those types of state and local workers whose jobs are routine, and for whom chance of advancement is scarce and wages are low.

It is likewise no accident that so many strikes have occurred among public school teachers. They form a special category that illustrates many of the problems of the classification system. A teacher is a graduate of a college or university; teachers are highly trained, skilled, and, in time, experienced. Public schools provide a hierarchy of promotions for teachers. A qualified person can become a specialist in teaching math, science, English, or some other subject and thus be promoted to a position supervising and training other teachers. A teacher can be promoted to assistant principal, principal, other administrative posts, and, once in a while, to superintendent of schools. The latter position may pay as much as fifty thousand dollars a year.

The plain fact, however, is that there are few opportunities for advancement among teachers. There are fewer than for policemen, for example, since the public school has nothing comparable to the ranks of sergeant, lieutenant, and captain. Therefore, under the existing situation, the vast majority of teachers remain at the lowest classification in the system. To keep pace with the rising cost of living, they depend upon annual increments in salary or a general pay increase for all teachers.

For the last quarter of a century there has been widespread agitation among teachers—and among the parents

Students in Minneapolis sit and watch their striking teachers.

and public who support them—for pay scales that are commensurate with the education, ability, and tasks of the job. There have also been more work stoppages by teachers than by any other type of public employees.

A paradoxical situation exists among large groups of public employees whose work is unskilled or semi-skilled, but is extremely vital. There is a body of knowledge and experience involved in doing any job, but after an initial period of training there is a basic routine involved in such jobs as collecting refuse, sorting and delivering mail, operating key-punch and other business machines.

Although the work may be relatively easily learned, compared to the training of engineers, scientists, and teachers, it is nonetheless vital. If anything, it is *more* vital. Much greater hardship occurs if a sanitation man does not collect garbage, if mail is not delivered, or if social security checks are not prepared than if teachers strike or an engineer fails to show up for work. The simple fact of the importance of their work is not lost on the host of workers in the lower classifications. They are demanding to be paid on the basis of the *importance* of their work, not on the *skill* involved.

Another cause of labor unrest among public workers has been the lessening appeal of the security that government employment has always offered. When civil service reform became a reality, job security became a major attraction. It was extremely difficult to fire a worker. Presidents, governors, and mayors might come and go, but the civil servant remained on his job. He might receive low wages, and his work might be routine and less than inspiring, but he got a paycheck when workers in private industry were pounding the pavement in search of a job, were laid off, or were standing in breadlines to feed their families. And, after a certain number of years on the job, he received a pension in his old age.

THE LIMITS OF DEFIANCE

Throughout most of American history the need for security was of undoubted importance. The American brand of capitalism made the United States the richest, most industrially powerful country in the world and created a large middle class, but there was a price to be paid—the more or less regular depression, the cycle of "boom or bust." Unshackled, undisciplined capitalism regularly resulted in an overproduction of goods, a surplus on the market, and a lowering of prices. Factories slowed down production and laid off workers to endure the decline in business. The loss of earnings by workers reduced consumers' buying power and prolonged the "bust." Eventually, however, inventories would dwindle, factories would increase production, workers would be rehired, more money would be in circulation, and there would be a "boom" for a few years. But every worker soon learned that the boom was temporary and would surely be followed by a bust. The civil servant knew it, too. He took less in the boom because he was sure of more, or at least something, during the bust.

Any American over the age of forty can remember the last of the busts, the Great Depression, which began in 1929 and lasted for about ten years, ending only with the outbreak of World War II. To combat this worst of all American depressions, the New Deal administration of Franklin D. Roosevelt enacted a host of programs aimed at ending forever the cycle of booms and busts. Many of the programs are still in operation, including social security, which provides pensions for retired persons and support for widows, orphans, and the handicapped; public welfare for the indigent; unemployment compensation for persons laid off, fired, or unable to find work; the Federal Reserve System to regulate banks, interest rates, and the amount of money in circulation; Federal Deposit Insurance to protect people from losing their savings; the Security and Exchange Commission to guard against wild speculation and corrupt practices on the stock exchanges; subsidy programs for farmers and many businesses; protection of labor unions; and regulation of nearly everything.

The era of "big government" began with the New Deal and has been continued and intensified at every level of government, bringing increased regulation and taxation, as well as stupendous increases in the number of government employees. Since the New Deal, the federal government, assisted by the states and cities, has attempted to regulate the economy to prevent another bust. Through regulation of business and labor practices, influence on wages and prices, taxation, appropriations, control of banking, and many other means, Congress and a succession of presidents have transformed the American economy from *laissez-faire* capitalism to state-controlled capitalism.

The effort has been amazingly successful. Since 1940, the United States has had only a few mild business turndowns, for which a new word, *recession*, had to be coined. As of now, a full-fledged bust is still only a memory of the middle-aged and elderly.

Perhaps the controlled economy has worked too well. In the decade of the 1960's, the United States experienced an immense boom, with ever-increasing production and demand for goods and services, all fueled by large profits, record wages, high government spending amidst reduced taxes, and an insatiable appetite for the "good life." Beginning in 1969, the federal government began applying the brakes to the economy to ward off a runaway inflation that could lead to another bust.

This is not intended as a lesson in economics. Rather, the intention is to show that since the New Deal, and particularly in the 1960's, the security of government employment has been considered less of an advantage than it was in the past. This is simply because with a controlled economy there is less of a need for this type of security.

The security of government work has been further eroded by the increased security of nongovernment work. Most industries make provisions for the retirement of employees, and, unlike most governments, often pay the full cost of pensions without any deductions from workers' wages.

The interest in security has waned, too, because it is easier for the average American to provide for his own retirement. Social security benefits were increased 15 percent in 1969, making comfort in old age more accessible for retired people. Many private insurance companies offer retirement plans that permit workers to provide for their old age during years of peak earnings.

Conversely, enthusiasm for the security offered by government employment has been dampened by cutbacks in federal employment. A government worker cannot be fired without "cause," which for practical purposes means he can be fired only for illegal acts or moral turpitude. But his job can be eliminated by abandoning the program in which he works or through simple budget cuts. In 1970, tens of thousands of engineers and scientists were eliminated from government payrolls by cuts in the budgets of the National Aeronautics and Space Agency and the Department of Defense. Many of these people had held some of the most "glamorous" positions in government. Partly for that reason many are finding it difficult to find jobs in private industry. An expert in developing plans for recovering astronauts from space would have great difficulty finding a comparable position in private industry.

Engineers and scientists are not the only workers feeling the pinch of reduced employability. School enrollments have leveled off and in some places declined. While there have not been extensive reports of teachers being laid off, many university graduates trained to be teachers are having a difficult time finding the work for which they were trained. There are fifteen thousand "extra" social science teachers, for example.

For all these reasons, the "security" of government employment has lost some of its appeal. In fact, the federal government has been downplaying the importance of job security for quite some time. Emphasis has been on high salaries, career advancement, and stimulating work. This is, in part, a reflection of government demand for skilled, professional employees, who until recently, at least, were less interested in security than career development.

Government may be able to make such an appeal to highly skilled and professional men, but it is quite another matter to state such a case to the millions of government employees who are in the lower grades and likely to remain there. With the lure of security diminished, they want what every other worker wants—to earn enough money for the necessities of life as well as the luxuries that most Americans consider necessities.

It is not an exaggeration to state that the typical American worker wants a home of his own or a decent apartment filled with modern furniture and appliances, a functioning automobile, and sufficient funds for plentiful food, medical care, insurance, serviceable if not fashionable clothing, an enjoyable vacation, with enough money left over to have some fun, send the children through college, and retire gracefully.

Achieving these goals is not very easy on the median family income in the United States of about nine thousand dollars a year. For the family of a public employee to do this on a salary of five, six, or seven thousand dollars a year is grossly more difficult.

Government workers in the lower classifications want higher salaries. They are agitating, threatening to strike, and striking to get them.

At this point you may be recalling that it is supposedly a policy of the federal government to pay salaries equal to those paid by private industry. That is true, but there are difficulties with the policy that are important causes of labor turmoil among public employees.

First, simply making a comparison between public and private employment can be difficult. Although there would be no difficulty comparing the wages of welders or boilermakers, registered nurses or engineers, to whom are the wages of a policeman to be compared? There are plant guards and private detectives, but they are relatively few and the work is not comparable.

Perhaps more obvious are firemen. The number of firemen hired by private employers is so low as to be totally neglected by statisticians. To whose wages can those of a firefighter be compared? A similar statement could be made about sanitation workers. Comparison is largely futile.

Thus, it may be said that a government policy of paying comparable wages may have validity among skilled and professional workers, but not among the workers in the lower grades, where most of the agitation occurs and among those occupations that form a large percentage of the employees of local government.

Second, labor leaders, economists, and other experts have predicted that major disputes over wages in private industry will take place in the 1970's. Many of the workers who fought labor's major battles in the 1920's, 1930's, and

1940's have retired. A younger generation of workers, few of them having memories of the Great Depression, are agitating for an *immediate* salary increase to make their wages commensurate with the nation's prosperity and high cost of living. Even if it were possible to equalize the salaries of all public workers with those in private industry, accomplishing this would mean large increases in public payrolls.

Third, and most important, the government's machinery for granting pay raises is rather cumbersome. The salaries of federal employees are set by Congress. At best it takes weeks for Congress to enact a pay raise bill. As a practical matter, Congress lags a year behind in "equaling" the pay of private industry. In a time of inflation, this lag keeps federal workers underpaid in comparison with private jobholders.

At the state and local level the lag is even more important. Many state legislatures meet only every other year, necessitating at best a two-year lag. Worse, state and local governments are prohibited by state constitutions or by law from deficit spending. Budgets must balance; that is, the amount of money spent must equal the amount of money earned. And state and local governments are chronically short of money. Each year, the budget creates a fiscal crisis, with state legislators and city councilmen paring (sometimes butchering) expenditures to bring them into line with revenues. To grant a general pay increase to public workers means either an increase in taxes or an elimination of services that are considered essential.

The situation is different in the federal government. It does not have to balance its budget. It can sell bonds (borrow money) to make up a deficit. Indeed, one of the effects of the pay raises granted after the postal strike was the unbalancing of the budget carefully prepared by President Nixon. Economists lamented this as encouraging inflation.

But the problems of granting pay raises at the state and local levels are more complicated than just balancing the budget. In Maryland, for example, the Baltimore City Police Department is a *state* agency. The city police commissioner is appointed by the governor. Any raise for city policemen has to be voted by the state legislature—but paid for out of city revenues. Thus, two different legislative bodies, the city council and the state legislature, have to be convinced if policemen are to have bulkier pay envelopes. Similar situations exist in other states, with legislatures maintaining partial or total control over local government functions. A common practice is to tie local pension plans for public workers to state retirement plans. If a mayor tried to negotiate increased pension benefits as part of a general pay increase for public workers, he might have to seek state approval.

The fuzzy line between state and local authority is not the most serious problem. In many states all increases in taxes at the local level have to be submitted to the voters for approval.

The demand for pay raises is coming at a time when there is mounting evidence of a taxpayers' rebellion. Most states have at least some forms of taxation that must be submitted to the voters. The most common issue is school taxation. There has been a sharp increase in the number of defeated tax levies, particularly for schools. In the St. Louis, Missouri, area, voters of thirteen school districts defeated school levies, one of them five times. Residents of rural Crook County, Oregon, rejected a school levy four times, finally agreeing to a drastically reduced school expenditure. Wealthy taxpayers of Scarsdale, New York, who once bragged that theirs was the best school system in the nation, twice rejected tax levies before accepting a skeletonized school budget. Nearly every state has experienced voter turndowns of school spending. In 1963, school bond issues passed 73 percent of the times they were offered to the voters. In 1969, slightly more than half were passed.

The voter rebellion against school taxation has occurred despite the severe penalties the turndown entails. Schools in Youngstown, Ohio, a state which perhaps leads all others in taxpayer rebellion, had to close early in a recent year for lack of funds. Many other school districts have been forced to take similar actions, or to lower teacher salaries, eliminate purchases of books and equipment, and even cut the curriculum to keep the schools open at all.

There are many reasons for the taxpayer rebellion. Voters may be poorly informed of the need for the taxation and how the money is to be spent. They may object to school officials or to educational policies and use the ballot as a way of expressing their feelings.

But a major reason for the rejections, certainly, is the rebellion against higher taxes. It is too complex a subject to describe in detail here, but in general the United States has a hodgepodge system of taxation. There are only four sources of tax revenues: taxes on incomes; sales; property; and an assortment of taxes, licenses, and fees imposed on products, services, and privileges, generally called "nuisance taxes."

Another cause of labor turmoil has been the concern of public employees over what might generally be labeled government policy. Postal workers agitated not only for pay raises, but also for postal reform that would make it easier for them to deliver the nation's mail efficiently.

Although this attitude exists among many groups of

Pittsburgh teachers strike in 1971 for better schools.

government workers, it seems strongest among teachers. In strike after strike, teachers have fought for improved education in the form of smaller classes, more books, and better classroom aids. Indeed, in 1970, teachers in Los Angeles settled a strike without any wage increases, but for increased appropriations for schools.

David Selden, president of the American Federation of Teachers, has stated this attitude most emphatically:

> What American schools need most is more teacher strikes. Instead of putting work stoppages by teachers in the same category as matricide and spitting on the flag, school board members and superintendents should be delighted when they have a group of educators who care enough about the schools and their own professional status to lay their jobs on the line in order to bring about improvements. . . .
>
> What is so terrible about a strike by teachers? The traditional answer is, "Think of the children!" Yet it is often more harmful to the children for teachers *not* to strike than it would be to close down the schools for a while. When New York City teachers were criticized for striking in April, 1962, Charles Cogen, then the union president, declared, "It is better for a child to lose a few days or weeks of schooling now than go through life handicapped by years of inferior education."
>
> . . . Should our children be taught by spineless economic illiterates lacking enough professional commitment to insist on decent school buildings, classes of teachable size, proper instructional materials, and salary schedules that can enable school systems to recruit teachers from the top of the graduating class instead of the bottom?

THE LIMITS OF DEFIANCE

Every strike, whether in the private or public sector, has some effect on policy. A strike by workers in private industry indirectly influences the price the company charges for its products. Labor-management negotiations in private industry customarily deal with wages and working conditions. They do not get into such matters as the quality of products manufactured.

When teachers strike for smaller classroom size, when welfare social workers leave their jobs demanding smaller case loads so they can deal with the problems of the poor more effectively, when air controllers demand improved equipment so they can better carry out their awesome responsibility of preventing air crashes, the repercussions on government policy extend beyond wages and working conditions.

How far can public employees go in striking to change policies? Can workers in the Department of Transportation strike against the decision to build the supersonic transport? Can employees of the Department of Defense strike because the president and Congress have reduced defense expenditures? Can workers in the State Department strike because of the war in Indochina? Such work stoppages may be said to be unthinkable, but so were all strikes by government workers just a few years ago.

CHAPTER 4

A Pattern of Neglect

AS EMPLOYEE dissatisfactions over wages, working conditions, and public policy began mounting, public officials reacted with gross neglect. That neglect is the biggest single cause of strikes by public employees. It was as if a tiger had been born in city halls and state houses across the land, but everyone insisted it was a lamb.

The neglect was so pervasive it is difficult to think of instances in which it did not occur. There was both a pattern to the neglect and a rationale. Public officials had long known of the dissatisfactions. Large numbers of public employees had belonged to professional associations and unions for decades. Leaders of these organizations regularly made known the workers' grievances in conferences with mayors, governors, and other officials, and in testimony to city councils, state legislatures, and Congress.

The problem was not that no one knew. The problem was that officials believed it was extremely difficult to do much about the workers' complaints and that there was little need to hurry.

THE LIMITS OF DEFIANCE

The neglect was not deliberate. Public officials were not disinterested in employee complaints. They listened and did what they could. The problem was that what they did was not enough. Workers would ask for a pay raise. Frequently they received nothing. At best they got only a fraction of what they asked. Appeals for better equipment to improve their ability on the job received much the same treatment.

Most officials failed the public employees only because they felt they had no other choice. There just was not enough tax revenue to go around. Municipalities were in a serious financial squeeze. While citizens were objecting to higher taxes, various community groups were demanding more expenditures for housing, welfare, traffic control, public transit, water and sewage service, education, crime prevention, and a host of other causes. City revenues were dwindling because the wealthiest citizens were moving to the suburbs and being replaced by poorer people who needed more services. And each time the property tax was raised, a few more urbanites moved to the suburbs—and business and industry followed. Economy became the civic watchword, and one way to economize was to ask more work from public employees while raising their wages as little as possible. This pattern went on for decades.

Comforting public officials in this neglect was the knowledge that it was against the law for public workers to strike. Indeed, prior to 1965, such strikes had seldom occurred. Workers might grumble, but they would just have to accept what was given to them.

In the face of this neglect, increasingly larger numbers of public employees began to organize and to demand that their organizations officially represent them in negotiations with city hall. These organizations had long existed. The Fraternal Order of Police was founded in 1915, the International Association of Fire Fighters in 1918, the Service Employees International Union in 1921, and the American Federation of State, County, and Municipal Employees in 1936. The National Education Association (NEA) was 108 years old in 1970, and the American Federation of Teachers was 54 years old. In addition to these national organizations, there were hundreds of local employee associations that had existed for years.

For the most part these organizations were considered "professional societies" or social groups. The National Education Association held an annual convention, as did state organizations, but these were devoted largely to improving teaching as a profession. Convention agendas dealt with such matters as teacher training and teaching techniques. NEA chapters proposed salary increases, but rarely got into the nitty-gritty bargaining for them. For the NEA to urge teachers to strike was out of the question.

Significant numbers of public employees had long belonged to formal labor unions, as distinct from associations. Blue-collar public workers belonged to various craft unions, such as the Teamsters, Bricklayers, or Laborers' Union. The American Federation of Teachers and the American Federation of State, County, and Municipal Employees were labor unions that sought to negotiate for public employees in the same manner as unions did in private employment.

The goals of public unions were not realized for a long time. Only a minority of public workers belonged to the unions, and attempts to bring in other workers were not notably successful. Besides, most governments refused to recognize or negotiate with labor unions. Such negotiations were considered an interference with the "sovereignty" of government. Government governed. It did not bargain with employees. It told them what to do.

THE LIMITS OF DEFIANCE

But labor unions were knocking at the door, demanding to represent their members. The professional associations, well aware of the complaints of their members, grew more militant in seeking higher wages and improved working conditions. It became difficult to tell the difference between an association and a union.

The door to unionism among public employees opened in February, 1962, with the historic White House Executive Order 10988. President John F. Kennedy gave federal employees the "right, freely and without fear of penalty or reprisal, to form, join and assist any employee organization or to refrain from any such activity." His order also granted these organizations the right to bargain with public officials concerning "grievances, personnel policies and practices, or other matters affecting general working conditions of employees in the unit." This limited bargaining right did not apply to any labor organization that failed to pledge not to strike against the government. Nor were the organizations allowed to bargain over such matters as wages or public policy. Wages were determined by Congress; policy was the prerogative of the president and his appointed officials.

President Kennedy's order opened the floodgates for unionism among public employees. His order applied only to federal workers, but almost immediately organizations in state and local governments demanded similar rights.

Membership in labor and labor-like unions skyrocketed. The International Association of Fire Fighters grew in membership from 87,000 in 1965 to nearly 150,000 in 1970. The number of locals increased as well. Membership in the American Federation of State, County, and Municipal Employees rose from 187,000 in 1962 to 371,000 in 1969, and here, too, there was a sharp rise in the number of local associations.

A PATTERN OF NEGLECT

The unions and associations began to become powerful —and learn how to use that power. Demands were issued for union recognition, collective bargaining rights, higher wages, and better working conditions. Strikes were threatened, job actions occurred, and finally full-blown strikes took place.

Strikers were taking action all over the country. But the most notoriety surrounded strikes in New York City, where welfare employees, transit workers, sanitation men, and teachers struck in defiance of state laws. Court orders were issued for the workers to return to their jobs and union leaders were jailed. Still, the strikes went on, ultimately to be settled for pay raises and agreement to other demands. There were few reprisals against the strikers.

The early strikes bore a message that was not lost on public workers all over the country. Anti-strike laws, court orders, and jailing of union leaders were hollow defenses. Even so large a city as New York became a paper tiger if a group of essential workers struck and remained off the job. The city of New York was not about to jail all of its teachers, sanitation men, transit workers, or welfare employees. Nor could it afford to fire these workers and hire and train new ones, or use troops to perform these services. Soldiers did not know how, nor did they want to do such jobs. The city had no choice but to sit down, bargain with the employees' union, and come to terms that would end the strike. Most importantly, New York City workers proved that by risking everything and striking, they got higher wages and better working conditions. Workers all over the country began to follow New York's lead. The number of strikes nationwide increased by the hundreds.

Incredibly, the neglect continued.

There is no better illustration of the pattern of neglect,

New York City experienced some of the early strikes in the recent surge of work stoppages by public employees. With public transportation at a standstill in 1966, workers walk across the Brooklyn Bridge into Manhattan.

even in the face of threatened strikes and the most impassioned pleas of union leaders, than in the postal strike of 1970.

The Post Office Department has been the stepchild of government for years. In theory it was expected to be self-supporting; that is, the revenues from stamps and other services were to equal the cost of running the department. This has hardly occurred in decades. Annually, the Post Office loses large sums of money on its operations, which are made up by Congressional appropriations. But the appropriations are seldom enough to provide adequate buildings and equipment, to pay wages that attract, keep, and satisfy postal employees, and to provide good mail service.

Everyone in the government knows this. Postmaster General Winton M. Blount stated in testimony to the Senate following the strike:

> The one fact that overshadows all others, of course, is that the Post Office Department has been in serious trouble for years. As early as 1967, the then Postmaster General, Mr. Larry O'Brien, candidly warned the American people that the Post Office Department was in a "race with catastrophe" and urged that extraordinary measures be taken to insure that the Post Office did not lose the race.

In response, President Lyndon B. Johnson appointed a commission to study the problems of the postal system. Its chairman was Frederick Kappel. Blount summarized its findings, and reported in 1968, in these words:

> The Kappel Commission found that the conditions of postal employment, particularly in our great urban

areas, left much to be desired. Quite apart from the question of pay, the Commission pointed out that the physical working conditions in many post offices were poor; that promotion opportunities in the postal system were limited; and that postal management was unable to make improvements that had been brought about many years before in the private sector through collective bargaining.

Blount quoted further from the Kappel Commission report:

> The system might be defensible, at least from the point of view of labor, if it produced decent working conditions and a satisfied work force. The tragedy is not only the frustration of management but the failure of the system to satisfy anyone.

When President Nixon took office, he sent a message to Congress urging postal reform. "For many years," the president said, "the postal worker walked a dead-end street." He went on:

> Today, particularly in our larger cities, postal workers labor in crowded, dismal, old-fashioned buildings that are little short of disgraceful. Health services, employee facilities, training programs and other benefits enjoyed by the worker in private industry and in other Federal agencies are, all too often, unavailable to the postal worker. In an age when machines do the heavy work for private companies, the postal worker still shoulders, literally, the burden of the nation's mail. That mail fills more than a billion sacks a year;

and the men and women who move those sacks need help.

Speaking after the strike, Blount called the prestrike pay rates "unconscionable." Speaking of the strike, he said:

> I am convinced . . . that what we witnessed . . . was a spontaneous demonstration of the fact that many of our long-time postal employees are simply fed up to the teeth with a system that no longer works and is no longer capable of responding effectively to their legitimate aspirations.

A question must be asked: If such views could be expressed *after* the strike, why was something not done *before* it? Indeed, why did the strike occur at all?

A most revealing answer, part of which did not appear in news coverage of the strike, came from James H. Rademacher, president of the National Association of Letter Carriers (NALC), largest of the postal unions. In September, 1970, he wrote his biennial report to his members. He detailed the events leading up to the strike, the strike itself, and its settlement.

Rademacher began by tracing the long history of postal service neglect, going back to the origins of the nation. He blamed the strike on more recent events.

> The 1970 work stoppage also had roots in the eight years of the Eisenhower Administration, during which the President saw fit to veto four pay bills. Although the final veto, in 1960, was overridden [by Congress], the end result of these lean years was that letter carriers fell tragically behind the economic parade.

Mailmen received a "decent" 11 percent pay increase in 1962, he said, but thereafter received minuscule increases of from 2 to 6 percent annually.

When Nixon became president in January, 1969, he asked for postal reform and made the statements quoted before. But there was a problem, which Rademacher explained as follows:

> When the Nixon administration embraced the concept of a postal corporation, the entire problem of an adequate pay structure for postal employees became hopelessly snarled in a political thicket. The administration made it quite clear that it would not tolerate a pay raise for postal employees unless it was accompanied by the creation of a postal corporation.

The Letter Carriers and other unions opposed creation of a postal corporation to replace the Post Office Department because the plan as originally presented bore no provisions for labor-management relations. Postal workers would have had no recourse to Congress in seeking wage hikes. Strikes were forbidden. Indeed, in the union's view, workers would be entirely dependent upon the postal corporation for any improvements.

This led to an impasse. As Rademacher expressed it:

> The NALC had sufficient power on Capitol Hill [Congress] to block the postal corporation in its original form, and the White House had sufficient power to block any pay bill.
>
> The only power to resolve this deadlock lay within the Executive Branch of the Government. But neither the White House nor the Post Office Department showed any inclination to exert this power.

Meanwhile, quite naturally, postal employees were becoming embittered at the inactivity of management and its unwillingness to grapple with their economic problems. They also, in the large metropolitan areas, where the cost of living is highest, saw city and state employees violate anti-strike laws and get away with it. School teachers, policemen, firemen, trash collectors, transit workers and others in similar essential jobs, hit the bricks and ended up with substantial pay increases, and with little or no penalties.

In June, 1969, Rademacher warned the president and Congress that "a postal strike was inevitable unless some constructive action was quickly forthcoming." On June 17, he told his entire membership to "cool it," for Congress seemed ready to take action. A wildcat walkout could threaten such progress.

Congress with maddening stubbornness continued to drag its heels. It was not until October 14 that the House of Representatives got around to passing a pay bill that would have given a 5.4 percent increase effective October 4, 1969. . . .

During the debate, the Republican leadership in the House of Representatives read a letter from the President . . . promising that, in the interest of curbing inflation, he would veto such a bill.

In the Senate, meanwhile, the Post Office Committee was determined to tie a pay increase to Post Office reform, which the unions opposed. As Rademacher expressed it, "Postal employees, obviously, were not going to wait all that time for added pay when their families were literally going without enough on which to survive."

THE LIMITS OF DEFIANCE

On December 4, 1969, the Senate Post Office Committee reported out a bill that Rademacher called a "nasty little parody" of the House bill. It would have given postal workers a 4 percent increase on January 1, 1970, and another 3 percent in July.

Rademacher said postal workers viewed this as a "complete betrayal." He said it took all the efforts of the union leadership to avoid a widespread wildcat strike during the Christmas rush.

On December 18, 1969, President Nixon invited Rademacher to the White House. The postal reform bill was revised so that the letter carriers could accept it. It called for compulsory arbitration of labor disputes. This progress was quickly short-circuited, first by "jealousy" among other postal unions that had not been consulted by the president, and then by members of Congress who had not been consulted either. The union president stated:

> The Democratic leadership in Congress was determined that the President would not get the credit for either reforming the Post Office or granting a pay raise to the postal employees. This impasse lasted, without any action by Congress, through the first two and a half months of 1970. The postal employees were becoming more and more impatient, and more and more angry at the way they were being victimized by political circumstances beyond their control.

Not until March 12, 1970, did the House Post Office and Civil Service Committee send to the floor a bill that created a Postal Corporation and granted a 5.4 percent increase retroactive to January 1.

As Rademacher expressed it, "It was all too late." Members of Branch 36 in New York City voted to strike. The wildcat walkout spread until one out of every five postal employees was off the job. Rademacher explained:

> The pent-up anger and frustration of hungry and sorely betrayed postal employees were breaking through the dams of self-restraint in almost every area of the nation.

It must be remembered that it was a wildcat strike. Union leaders had not called the strike but rather had urged the men not to strike and the workers had walked out anyway. Union officials had lost control.

At this time, Rademacher prepared a resolution demanding that negotiations begin immediately, or the union would call an official and nationwide strike Monday, four days away.

> The attitude of the Postmaster General was almost incredible. . . . He insisted that the strike was my affair far more than it was his. He refused to enter any kind of negotiations until the men were back to work. The men, on the other hand, were insisting that negotiations must begin before they would go back in.

Rademacher prepared a message to be sent to all union locals at 11 A.M. on Friday, March 20.

> It is my observation that despite my efforts and those of the NALC Executive Council to terminate the wildcat strikes that are now in progress, current developments make it likely that there will be no postal service anywhere in the United States on Monday, March 23. Then what happened?

At five minutes to eleven, just 300 seconds before

United States Army troops sort the mail in New York, when workers there held out, after the 1970 postal strike was settled in the rest of the nation.

deadline, Secretary of Labor Shultz did call me and indicate he was willing to begin negotiations.

The NALC Executive Council voted in favor of negotiating with the administration but insisted that concrete results would have to be achieved within five days. With that, most of the postal workers returned to their jobs, although members of Branch 36 in New York remained defiant. After President Nixon called out federal troops to deliver the mail in New York, the workers gave in.

At 2 P.M. on March 25, negotiations began. Rademacher reported:

> We all worked practically around the clock at the arduous task of negotiation. I am the first to admit that I was disappointed at first in the pace of the negotiations. There was a frustrating lack of urgency on the part of Government negotiators. There was a maddening tendency on the part of some to quibble over unimportant details, to try to blow minor points into major issues. There was, at first, too much complacency on the part of a few key people—a feeling that now the men had returned to their jobs, they would stay in them and the danger of further outbreaks was past. I did everything in my power to disabuse them of this idea. . . .

Failing, and his "patience exhausted," Rademacher prepared a statement to be read on national television in which the union would call a national strike the following Monday, April 6.

> I can report that the effect of this statement, and my obvious determination to make it, had an elec-

trifying effect on the negotiations on both sides of the table. Immediately, the atmosphere changed, and the package we finally developed began to take shape before our eyes.

In the end, the postal workers won a 14 percent wage increase plus fringe benefits. The union had wanted only 12 percent. A delighted Rademacher reported, "We had won more than we had to concede."

Rademacher's fascinating narrative reveals several things of paramount importance. First, everyone in the federal government knew of the gross dissatisfactions of postal employees. Indeed, they had been warned of a possible strike. Second, the pattern of neglect that had been going on for decades continued. Postal workers were consistently frustrated in obtaining a pay raise. Third, not until the strike occurred did action begin. Fourth, once the men had returned to their jobs and negotiations began, a leisurely pace was still maintained. Fifth, not until a strike was again threatened did the negotiations bear fruit. Sixth, and most important, government officials, negotiating under the gun of a threatened strike, gave up more than would have been necessary had some sort of meaningful negotiation taken place long before.

The postal problem was clearly a product of neglect. Not all public strikes are rooted in neglect, but it is a major factor in many. Indeed, most of the solutions offered for the problem of public strikes involve some system for eliminating the neglect and coping with employee complaints in an orderly fashion.

CHAPTER 5

Strikes in Three Cities

IN 1967, THE city of Detroit, Michigan, had a most serious "epidemic" of the "blue flu." It was not a new, exotic disease, but a job action by Detroit policemen seeking a wage increase. The story of the slowdown reveals a great deal about both the nature of the labor problem among public workers and the difficulties in resolving them.

In January, 1966, the Detroit Police Officers Association, recognized as the official bargaining unit for the Motor City's thirty-eight hundred men in blue, asked for a $1,665 across-the-board pay increase. This would have raised their maximum base salary to $9,000. Negotiations went on for several months. Finally, the city's Labor Relations Director recommended that the city grant the $1,665 increase. Instead, the city budget for that year allowed only a $1,000 increase.

In September, 1966, the police union requested that maximum base salaries be raised the following year from $8,335 to $10,000. The city replied that it could not negotiate salaries for the next year until it determined how much money was available for salary increases. Fruitless negotiations continued for some time. Finally, the union threatened strike action. One union official is alleged to have said, "We are going to hit you with the blue flu."

There was the usual background to these feelings. Other public employees, particularly teachers, in Michigan had struck and obtained higher wages. Police in Pontiac, near Detroit, had come down with "instant flu" and obtained a sizable wage increase. At the same time the Detroit force was undermanned, which was partly attributable to low salaries. Finally, the police officer's image in the city had declined, particularly among ghetto residents. The policeman tended to feel that if he was going to be disliked, he might as well be paid adequately for doing his job while people disliked him.

In May, 1967, with negotiations getting nowhere, Detroit policemen began a "ticket slowdown." The city was receiving substantial revenues from traffic and parking tickets written by policemen—as much as $7 million a year. Patrolmen simply began to write fewer tickets, and within a matter of days, the number written dropped by 60 percent. Mayor Jerome Cavanagh denounced the action as "irresponsible," and the police commissioner ordered a stop to the slowdown. The policemen's reply was to write even fewer tickets. By the middle of June, ticket-writing was down 80 percent.

The police commissioner reacted with a "get tough" policy. He suspended some patrolmen and reassigned men from patrol cars to foot patrol beats.

The policemen retaliated with the "blue flu." Increasing numbers of men began calling in "sick." Soon, a fourth of the force was either "sick," disabled, or suspended. While the mayor demanded that the policemen return to work, the head of the union said that the mayor was responsible for the slowdown because he had attended none of the bargaining sessions. A name-calling impasse had been reached, leaving Detroit with crippled police services.

Into this situation stepped a commission of leading citizens headed by the Right Reverend Richard Emrich, the Episcopal Bishop of Michigan. Both the mayor and the police union agreed to meet with the commission. A truce was arranged; the sick-out would be called off and negotiations would go on for ten days. If an agreement could not be reached in that time, an impartial fact-finding panel would be called in. The city and police union agreed to do "all in their power" to put the panel's recommendations into effect as soon as possible.

Ten days of negotiations produced no results, and the issues were placed in the hands of fact finders selected by the Emrich Commission. The panel's work was interrupted in July and August, 1967, by the riots in Detroit's black ghettos. Because of the need for full police services during this emergency, all charges against suspended patrolmen were dropped.

In February, 1968, the fact finders, all expert and experienced men, returned a report that shocked city officials by recommending that the ten thousand dollar wage sought by the policemen be granted. The panel found the policemen's job to be so hazardous and demanding, and the department's wages so low that "the plain truth . . . which emerges . . . is that the Detroit police department faces a manpower crisis. . . ." Only higher wages could resolve it.

Moreover, the fact finders declared that the city could afford the pay raise. It had the power to raise substantially more money from property taxes, to cut back its capital improvement program, to make use of surplus funds in various city agencies, and even to borrow money if necessary. The commission denied the city's allegations that it lacked legal authority to reopen the existing budget to provide more money for policemen. In its most telling statement, the panel said, ". . . the city's inability to pay increased police salaries is in some measure a self-imposed inability."

Policemen were delighted, city officials aghast. The latter said the panel did not truly understand city problems and warned that a pay increase for policemen would lead to the reopening of the city's contracts with other workers and the granting of "me-too" wage increases.

Negotiations began on the basis of the fact finders' report and an agreement was reached. The blue flu epidemic ended. But, as the city had warned, contracts with seventy-nine other unions had to be renegotiated at a cost of more than $9 million to the city. As one city official put it, "We tried to convince the fact finders that this would happen, but we couldn't get them to listen."

A somewhat different situation occurred in San Francisco early in 1970. The state of California had a law which, while banning strikes by public employees, required local officials to "meet and confer" with union leaders. Such conferences took place, and the municipality's Civil Service Commission sent to the Board of Supervisors a recommended pay increase for fifteen thousand city employees, exclusive of policemen, firemen, teachers, municipal railway drivers, and craft union members, who were all covered under separate agreements. The commission recommended that the "miscellaneous" workers be granted a 7.5 percent pay hike, which would cost the city an estimated $9.5 million.

Mayor Joseph Alioto, who had been elected with strong backing from the city's labor unions, threatened to veto such an increase. He cited a "taxpayer revolt" as his reason and was able to list considerable evidence of the revolt. In the previous election, three bond issues on the ballot had been defeated by a wide margin, and two members of the Board of Supervisors were defeated on a spending issue. Moreover, letters, telegrams, and other messages coming into city hall indicated overwhelming public opposition to the pay raise.

Under such influences, the Board of Supervisors cut the pay increase to 5 percent, which would cost the city $4.8 million. The board accomplished this by eliminating a pay increase for city workers the following year, 1970–71. The annual 5 percent "increment" in employee salaries had been going on since 1943. The board decided to stop it. Thus, the board and the mayor offered workers an immediate raise, but nothing for the following year.

Union leaders protested and threatened to strike. The mayor was adamant. "You can't get blood out of a turnip," he said. "The property taxpayer has had it." Negotiations failed, and on Friday, March 13, city employees struck.

The strike was called by four city unions, the Service Employees International Union (the members of which perform custodial and maintenance work in public buildings), the Nurses Association, the City and County Technical Engineers Union, and the Stationary Engineers Union. They were joined by four other unions, the Teamsters, Longshoremen, teachers, and the Municipal Railway Operators. The latter four unions were not involved in the pay dispute. They had already settled their contracts, but they joined the walkout in sympathy. The effect was to immobilize the city. Schools were closed. Buses, streetcars, and cable cars stopped running. Hospital workers refused to cross picket lines. Virtually all municipal services, except police and fire protection, halted. The mayor said "chaos was near." The only saving grace was that this

Municipal services in San Francisco came to a halt during a strike by city workers. Above, a striking employee stands in front of an idled cable car. Right, cars are parked on streetcar tracks not in use.

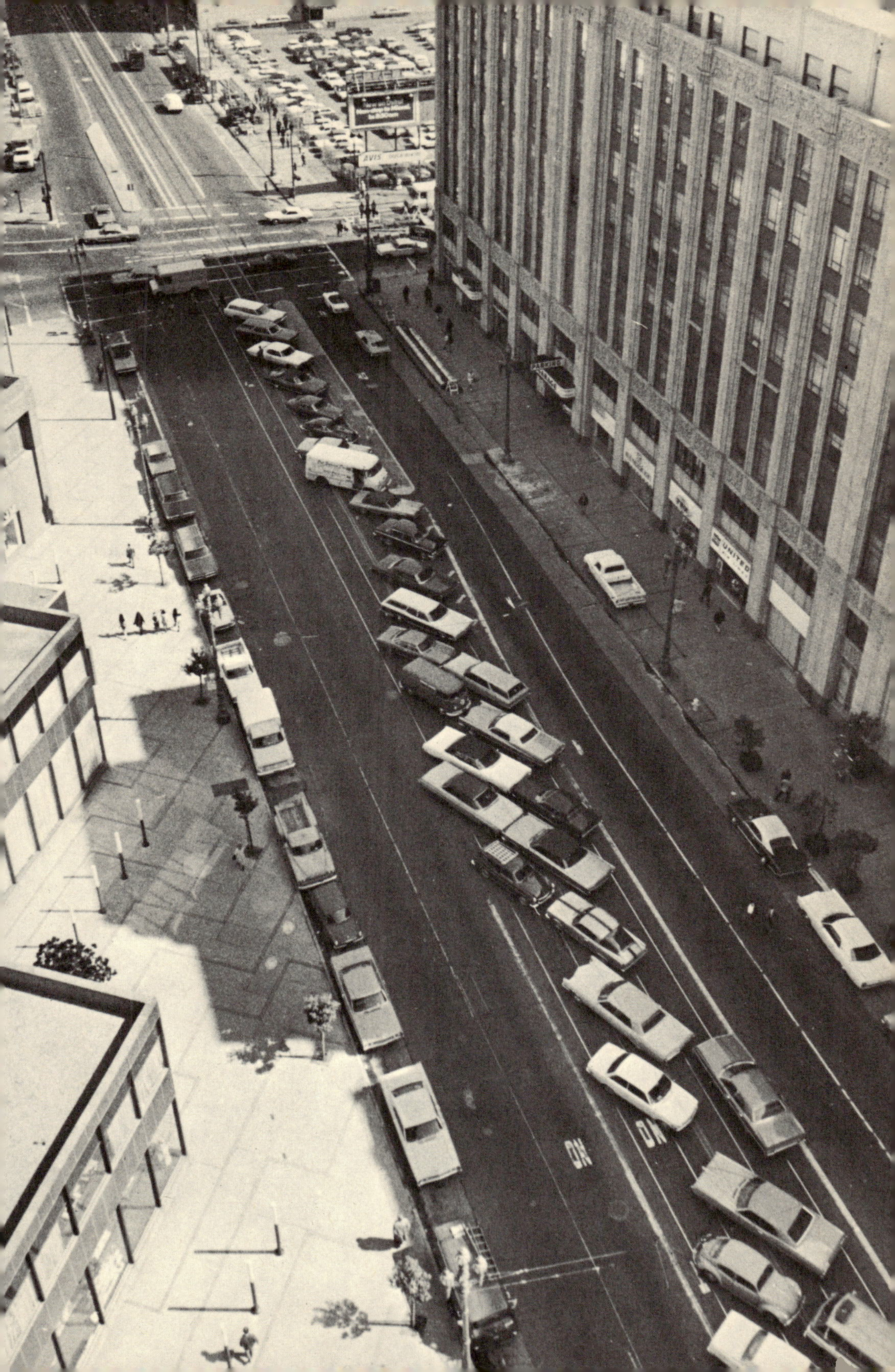
AVIS
UNITED

occurred during a weekend, when there is less of a demand for city services.

With the strike underway, both city officials and union leaders moved energetically to end it. Both sides were under extreme pressure to solve the issue. For political as well as humane reasons the mayor could not allow the strike to go on. Nor did union members want to politically embarrass the mayor, who was personally popular among them. Furthermore, the sympathy strikers, who had nothing at stake in the bargaining, pressured the "miscellaneous" workers to settle.

A negotiating team was rounded up and intensive negotiations began. The problem, in the political climate of the city, was to work out a settlement that would be acceptable to the workers, yet allow the mayor to honor the taxpayers' revolt. In short, both sides entered the negotiations seeking a way for everyone to "save face."

The negotiations went on all weekend. Finally, a break came when union accountants, poring over the city's financial books, discovered that the Civil Service Commission had overestimated the size of the pay increase by about $1 million. The mayor, faced with the threat of a spreading strike by private industry workers, capitulated. A compromise was worked out giving the employees a 5 percent increase immediately as well as retaining the 5 percent annual increment.

A much less serious, but far more acrimonious strike occurred in Cleveland, Ohio, in the fall of 1969. It was a clash of personalities, race, and politics that seemed to defy solution.

Cleveland was the first major city in the nation to elect a black mayor, Carl Stokes. At the time of the strike, he was facing a challenging reelection campaign against a white opponent. A major source of Stokes's political support, in addition to black voters, came from unions. During his term in office, Stokes had been progressive in handling city labor problems in a state that has one of the most stringent laws governing public strikes. It imposes severe penalties on strikers and does not require a city to even recognize a public employee union. Nevertheless, Stokes did recognize the union. By signing "memorandums of agreement" with fourteen unions representing thirteen thousand employees, he, in effect, permitted the unions to bargain on wages and working conditions. A result was general labor peace among municipal employees, with whom Stokes enjoyed considerable popularity.

A gadfly in this situation was Clarence King, chief steward of Local 100 of the American Federation of State, County, and Municipal Employees. Both King and most of the workers in his thirteen-hundred-member local are black. The local included water service and sewer maintenance employees, airport safety workers, and some members of various other departments. King had had a stormy relationship with city officials. He had been suspended by the city several times for alleged violations of civil service rules. He replied that the city's utilities director was pursuing a "personal vendetta" against him. Whichever allegations were true, there had been several wildcat strikes by members of Local 100.

The situation came to a head in August, 1969. Each side has presented conflicting views of the dispute, but as near as an impartial person can discern, it began with the conversion of a city water truck into a supply truck. This vehicle was delivering materials to an installation when King placed himself in front of it and stopped it. He objected to the truck's being driven by a member of the Teamsters Union. He insisted it was a water truck and should be driven by a member of Local 100. He maintained that he had been trying to discuss the problem with various city officials for over a week, but without success.

Officials of Local 100 and the Teamsters Union met with city officials on the spot. An agreement was reached—a Teamster would drive the truck, but a member of Local 100 would ride with him as a helper. Just as all the parties were preparing to shake hands, King was called to the phone and told that he was suspended from work pending the bringing of discharge proceedings for stopping work at a city installation.

A major squabble ensued, much of it before television cameras. Charges flew. Union officers claimed a city official said he was "going to break the union." This was denied. King charged the utilities director with conducting a personal vendetta. This, too, was denied.

Mayor Stokes came to the installation to meet personally with King and other union officials, the city's director of personnel, and utilities director. The union took the position that it would accept a suspension of King, but not his discharge or his transfer from the installation to another post in the city. This seemed acceptable, but, according to the union, after the mayor left, the utilities director insisted upon King's discharge. Union officials walked out of the meeting. The next day they struck.

The strike itself was not a serious disruption of city affairs. But two events occurred that inflamed passions. The president of Local 100 went on television and demanded the resignation of the utilities director. Lines hardened. It became a personal battle between King and the director over who would be fired. Then, according to city officials, King and other members of Local 100 appeared at the utilities department and forced two hundred clerical workers to leave the building by threatening them. One worker claimed he was punched in the jaw.

Mayor Stokes then took a firm stand. He ordered policemen to guard all utility installations and denounced King for "muscle tactics" and "terrorist tactics." King and two other union officials were arrested as they walked out of the room in which King's discharge proceedings were underway.

Thus, what had begun as a dispute over a driver of a converted truck had blown up into a first-class political and racial issue. Mayor Stokes, facing reelection, was in the middle. On the one hand, he faced the loss of support among black voters because of his opposition to a black labor leader. He could be accused of courting white votes at the expense of black workingmen. On the other hand, if he gave in to King, Stokes could be accused by white voters of playing favorites on the basis of race and allowing muscle tactics to go unpunished. Whatever position he took, however he solved it, the mayor risked being accused of operating on a double standard.

Into the impasse strode Jerry Wurf, president, and other national officials of the American Federation of State, County, and Municipal Employees. Wurf, a highly experienced union official, was also "in a bind." It is axiomatic that a national union official must support a union local. Without such support, national officers cannot enlist the support of the rank and file that elects them. In this case, Wurf could have called upon other AFSCME locals to support Local 100. As a member of the executive board of the AFL-CIO he could have asked private unions to support his members. The result could have been a greatly broadened, vastly more serious strike in Cleveland.

But to do this would have meant turning the black workers of Cleveland against a black mayor. Such union actions would have, at the least, aggravated a precarious racial situation in Cleveland. As a national union official put it,

"We don't want to be in the position of the white leadership of this union being responsible for the defeat of a black mayor; it's as simple as that."

Wurf agreed to a proposal that had been discussed for several days—bringing in an impartial person to mediate the dispute. The choice was Willoughby Abner, an experienced, highly respected arbitrator. He had been affiliated with the United Auto Workers union and had been special assistant to the director of the Federal Mediation and Conciliation Service. Later, he became vice-president of the American Arbitration Association and head of its National Center for Dispute Settlement. In addition to these credentials, Abner had one other asset: he was black.

Even as Abner entered the dispute, the issue was hardening. King sought the full backing of the Cleveland AFL-CIO organization. He received an endorsement for the strike, but admitted it was "lukewarm at best." The city countered by getting a pledge from the other thirteen unions representing city workers not to honor Local 100's picket lines. Then Stokes went on television to say the issue was not Clarence King but "whether a union has the right to accomplish its objectives, no matter how unreasonable or arbitrary, by resorting to illegal wildcat strike actions and other illegal pressures." Stokes added that "now the city has no choice but to stand firm and insist that the contract procedures be followed. If we fail in this dispute, then our 1968 negotiations were worthless and we might as well throw away all of our labor contracts." Certainly, Willoughby Abner had his work cut out for him.

He called a meeting between himself, the union, and the city officials. It turned acrimonious. Charges were hurled. King spoke bitterly of the city's accusation that he was "irresponsible."

Abner broke off the talks and huddled with the parties separately. He met with King, man to man. What happened in their discussion, as well as the others, was private. It will not be made public until one of the parties involved chooses to do so. Gradually, through constant talk, Abner began to move Local 100 and city officials closer to an agreement. For example, the issue came to be not whether King should be discharged, but how long he should be suspended.

To resolve this situation, Abner arranged a meeting between Stokes and Wurf, the latter celebrated for his dynamism and quick temper. The two quarreled and both got up to leave. Willoughby Abner physically barred the door and forced both Wurf and Stokes to remain in the room.

When they later emerged smiling, the strike was over. The union had agreed to honor its no-strike pledge to the city. King would be suspended for a month, half of which had been served during the strike. The city would do its best to live up to contract agreements with the union. Although when it was over, the solution seemed simple, the acrimony between Local 100 and city officials remained.[1]

These three strikes (many others might have been chosen) illustrate a pattern of work stoppages. It is a mosaic of bitterness, conflict, personal animosity, hardened positions, racial overtones, political considerations, and desperate, makeshift, last-minute negotiations after a work stoppage is in progress. In Detroit and San Francisco, where wages were the principal issue, workers engaged in

---

[1] For a fuller account of the strikes in Detroit, San Francisco, and Cleveland, read *Work Stoppages: A Tale of Three Cities*, which journalist John A. Grimes wrote for the Labor-Management Relations Service, 1612 K Street, N. W., Washington, D. C. 20006.

stoppages after they received what they considered unreasonable offers that could not be improved through negotiations. City officials, faced with work stoppages that created close to intolerable conditions, were forced to agree to wage payments that they believed the city could not afford and that risked a taxpayer revolt.

These three strikes also illustrate a problem. No particular clairvoyance is required to project this situation into the future. Continued demand by workers for ever higher wages could result in one of two situations. The first could be a growing number of public strikes, which paralyze essential city functions. If private labor organizations support public employees by striking, their joint action could lead to general strikes with close to disastrous results. Second, by granting pay increases to avoid strikes, city officials could bring about extremely high taxation. If citizens refused to pay, municipal bankruptcy could result. Governments would be forced to resort to drastic cuts in both the number and quality of services provided. If bankruptcy did not occur, there would be a risk of runaway inflation, which could conceivably lead to another economic "bust."

Thus, both union leaders and public officials realize they are playing a high-risk game. Both agree that some form of solution must be found to the problem, although they disagree about what that solution should be.

Two main solutions are most commonly used. The first might be called the "hard line" approach. Stringent laws are passed declaring all forms of work stoppages illegal. Severe penalties are imposed on unions and workers who strike and the penalties are enforced.

The second suggested solution is to apply to the public sector the nation's long experience in the private sector.

Public labor problems would be handled in essentially the same manner as problems in private industry.

Alternate solutions are rather amorphous at the moment, but a search is on for an entirely new method of handling labor disputes in the public sector.

Both the tried and the untried approaches will be discussed separately.

CHAPTER 6

Strikes Are Illegal

STRIKES BY public employees are forbidden by the federal government and in every state save two, Hawaii and Pennsylvania. Even in those two states strikes are allowed only among certain types of employees and only after a long list of other remedies has been exhausted. In the federal government and in most states, the prohibition against strikes is based on public law. In other states, court rulings and opinions by attorneys general achieve the same result. Indeed, some judges have held that ancient English common law makes any public strike illegal.

The anti-strike provisions are backed by some harsh penalties. These penalties vary from state to state, but in general they are as follows:

    A. All strikers can be fired and lose their retirement benefits.
    B. Large fines can be imposed on a union calling a strike.

Striking firemen in Des Moines, Iowa, wait to pay fines of $100 each during a 1969 work stoppage.

C. Union leaders or anyone aiding and abetting a strike can be imprisoned and/or fined. In some cases individual workers can be imprisoned for striking.

D. A striking union can lose its recognition as an exclusive bargaining agent for its members. This means the government would refuse to recognize the union or to negotiate with it.

E. The union "checkoff" rights can be rescinded. The checkoff is the system by which employers withhold union dues from an employee's paycheck and turn them over to the union. The checkoff has been called the "lifeblood" of a union. Without it, unions find it extremely difficult to collect dues.

In addition to these rather common penalties, there is another with serious repercussions. The state of Ohio, under its Ferguson Act, outlawed pay raises for striking workers for one year. During that period of time, however, the city of Cincinnati granted a raise to workers following a strike, but an Ohio court ruled that the pay raise was contrary to state law. This ruling may have far-reaching importance. James Baird of the Labor Relations Management Service made this comment:

> If that [the Ohio court] decision holds up, and if the decision means that a city official may not grant a raise as the result of an illegal strike, the motivation for striking on the part of Ohio public employees may be greatly dissipated. Additionally, the general pressures to grant pay raises as a result of strikes may be lifted from the shoulders of that state's elected officials.

The penalties for striking are not just idle threats. In his report to his membership in 1970, James H. Rademacher, president of the National Association of Letter Carriers, explained why he was so hesitant to call a nation-wide postal strike. He listed these reasons:

- The NALC "would cease to exist as a recognized union" in the eyes of the government. All existing contracts could be immediately and automatically canceled. Seniority rights could end, and the NALC could be prohibited from representing its members.
- The Federal government could abandon all participation in the Civil Service Retirement Program. "Our members would have been entitled to get back from the Federal government the money they had invested in the program, and that is all."
- The government could withdraw all support of and participation in the health benefits and life insurance programs.
- Every striking worker could be fired.
- The checkoff could end and the union be driven into "instant bankruptcy."
- Courts could impose heavy fines on the national union and its local branches.

The union official listed another penalty that was "more important" than all the others.

In officially calling a national strike, I would have been technically guilty of an illegal act. In following my leadership, the National Association of Letter Carriers as an organization would have been guilty of a criminal act. Under the law, any individual or organization guilty of criminal behavior is automatically responsible for financial losses incurred by innocent bystanders as a result of such criminal action. Therefore, every business, financial or industrial institution which depends upon the mails for its economic well-being would have been quite free to sue the NALC for any loss it suffered as a result of our action. The suits resulting from such an action could have reached into the billions of dollars.

Rademacher said that at least two firms threatened to bring million-dollar suits against the union during the wildcat strike in March, 1970.

He also summed up all the penalties in these words:

> I did not accept election to the presidency of the NALC for the purpose of presiding over its dissolution. Several million valiant letter carriers, dead and gone, devoted their lives to the creation and development of the NALC as it now exists. More than 212,000 letter carriers today look to the NALC for support, protection and for their future welfare. It would have been criminally irresponsible for me to have thrown all this away in one angry and unreasoned gesture of defiance.

Most, perhaps all, leaders of unions of public employees advocate the lifting of no-strike laws, excepting only policemen and firemen. Unions demand the right to strike for public workers. And their leaders offer a variety of reasons for permitting the right to strike. Some of these will be discussed in the next chapter. But in the context of this discussion, it is important to remember that union leaders consider the no-strike laws to be ineffective. They cite the fact that strikes occur despite the ban against them.

There is logic to this view. Striking is perhaps an inalienable right. In a democratic society, men or women cannot be forced to work.

Empty patrol cars are a symbol of the ultimate strike during a job action by New York City policemen in January, 1971.

There is also history to back the contention that antistrike laws are unworkable. In its century-long turmoil over labor relations in the private sector, the nation discovered that strikes occurred despite legal bans against them, despite the firing of workers, despite the hiring of "scabs" to replace them. These efforts to prevent the strike led to violence between strikers, police, and soldiers. There were pitched battles in which both strikers and police were killed and wounded by the dozens. After these prolonged, bitter lessons, the nation achieved relative labor peace by legalizing strikes and establishing machinery to settle labor disputes. Labor leaders maintain that the United States should not repeat the dreadful past by outlawing strikes by public workers.

Labor leaders also contend the no-strike laws are unenforceable. They argue that the federal government would have incurred great expense and loss of service if it had fired the postal workers who struck in 1970 and sought to recruit and train replacements. Union leaders ask how a public school system could fire and replace its striking teachers, a city its police, fire, sanitation, and other workers.

Fining and jailing union leaders also fail to have much effect. Among the celebrated union leaders jailed were Albert Shanker, head of the United Federation of Teachers, and John J. De Lury, head of the sanitation men, in New York City. David Selden, national president of the American Federation of Teachers, was jailed during a strike in Newark, New Jersey. Union leaders argue that such penalties only harden the union opposition to a settlement and remove the leadership from negotiations. Imprisoning also introduces another issue into the dispute, the release of jailed officials and the demand that strikers not be penalized after a settlement.

STRIKES ARE ILLEGAL

A final labor argument against no-strike laws is that since the laws are unenforceable, keeping them on the books breeds contempt for the law and a climate in which laws are broken.

As persuasive as the unions' arguments against no-strike laws are, there is another side to the coin. Clearly, Rademacher's report to his membership shows that the severe penalties of the law kept him from calling a nationwide postal strike despite strong pressure from his membership to do so. It perhaps follows that no-strike laws are useful in dampening the enthusiasm of irresponsible labor leaders for a strike. The laws may be viewed as encouraging negotiation.

The "hard line" approach to labor disputes, based upon enforcing the laws, has been useful in ending strikes. A notable example occurred in West Virginia, where thirty-four hundred state road employees, organized by the Laborers Union of the AFL-CIO, struck. West Virginia had no law governing labor disputes by public workers. Moreover, state road workers were not included in the civil service system. The employees feared they would lose their jobs when Arch Moore, a Republican, replaced the Democratic governor. The workers tried to talk to the state road commissioner about wages, seniority, and other matters, but failed. A state official explained that the governor was barred by the state constitution from granting recognition and bargaining rights to unions.

The workers struck on March 3, 1969. A few days later there was a heavy snowfall. Moore asked the men to return to work to clear the roads. When they refused, he fired them all. Gradually, fifteen hundred of the strikers returned to work, presumably as new employees. The strike continued, but with diminishing effect. By September, the state had twenty-nine hundred men—mostly new employees—on its road force. The strike had failed. The hard line won.

The situation in West Virginia was perhaps unusual. The state lacked any sort of law. Unemployment there has been high for years, and unions are less militant than in other areas. Other union men, representing 44 percent of the labor force in the state, gave the road workers little support. This was in part a reflection of the long-standing antipathy between the United Mine Workers union, which is powerful in the state, and the AFL-CIO unions.

Some other examples of strikes in recent history that produced less than overwhelming success were a three-week strike by teachers in Florida, a strike by hospital workers in South Carolina, and the sanitation men's strike in Memphis, Tennessee, during which Dr. Martin Luther King, Jr., was murdered. These and many other strikes produced settlements, to be sure, but workers were far from satisfied with the results.

In general, most public strikes have been settled by the "soft line" approach. City officials bargain with strikers to reach a settlement. But in every strike, there has been a body of public opinion urging the use of the hard line. Jail the leaders, fine the union, fail to recognize the union, end the checkoff, fire the workers, call out troops to man the services. In short, don't give in to strikers.

Responsible labor leaders maintain that such an approach will lead only to the sort of violence that bloodied American labor relations for so long. Equally responsible "hard liners" reply that there are significant differences between labor relations in the private and public sectors, and that strikes by many types of public workers are so great a threat to public welfare and safety that they must be prohibited by law and the law enforced regardless of

The 1968 strike by sanitation workers in Memphis, Tennessee, lost some of its effect when the city used nonstriking workers and new employees to collect the city's garbage.

the consequences. Workers, it is argued, must accept other means of settling labor disputes short of a strike.

The argument over the right to strike, the hard line versus the soft line approach, is one of the paramount issues in public labor disputes. The issue is greatly complicated by the variety of state laws governing labor disputes. New laws and amendments to old ones are being passed by state legislatures every year. But as of 1970, the state laws were a hodgepodge. Half the states had no law at all. Others had laws governing only some public employees, omitting the rest. Some states had created special agencies to deal with labor disputes, while in other cases these matters were left to elected officials.

The variances in terminology from state to state are significant. There is a difference between having a "duty to negotiate" or being "required to bargain" and being "authorized to meet and confer" with workers. Also present are such terms as "having an obligation to negotiate," "required to confer," and "authorized to bargain." A number of states "require" written agreements, others "authorize" them, and still others ignore the subject.

There are also wide variances in who does the negotiating, bargaining, or meeting and conferring. Some states set up agencies, some use existing agencies, and others turn the matter over to local officials or state department heads. Procedures for recognizing unions similarly lack uniformity, as do those for breaking deadlocks.

Virtually every person who has investigated the problem of public labor disputes has found state legislation somewhat less than satisfactory—to make a deliberate understatement.

The differing state laws, as well as the lack of laws, may be viewed as evidence that hardly anyone can agree on the best legal solution to public employee labor problems.

There have been many studies of the problem by legislators, Congress, and commissions at every level of government. The divergent laws reflect the different opinions.

Three solutions are most often advocated. One was best stated in the report of the Advisory Commission on Intergovernmental Relations. A majority of its twenty-seven participants—including private citizens, United States senators and congressmen, federal government officials, governors, mayors, state legislators, and elected county officials—agreed that the "meet and confer in good faith approach" was the "most appropriate" in state and local governments. In this way, state and local officials would be required to consult union officials, but they would reach a decision on wages and other matters under dispute. Workers would be required to accept the decision under penalty of the law.

A minority of the commission dissented forcefully. Officials of the AFL-CIO denounced the report as a "backward" step.

A second solution was offered by the highly respected Twentieth Century Fund through its Task Force on Labor Disputes in Public Employment. A group of experts in public and private labor-management practices endorsed legislation calling upon "the public employer" to "meet and negotiate with the union" and reduce the agreement to writing.

In other words, two equally eminent bodies of men met, considered the problem, and recommended two different types of state laws, one to have public officials "meet and confer in good faith," the other that public officials have a "duty" to negotiate written agreements.

A third solution is being actively sought by the American Federation of State, County, and Municipal Employees. It has drafted and submitted to Congress a "model law," which, if enacted, would set uniform standards for labor-management relations all over the country. Many people agree upon the need for a uniform law, without agreeing to the terms prepared by the AFSCME. That law calls for collective bargaining, which brings us to organized labor's approach to the problem of public labor disputes.

CHAPTER 7

Are Public and Private Employers the Same?

ORGANIZED LABOR believes that the practices used in settling labor problems in private industry should be followed in solving disputes among government workers.

In report after report, speech after speech, labor leaders make it clear that they can see no significant difference between private and public labor disputes. In describing the problem they use the words "labor" to describe public employees and "management" to refer to elected or appointed officials—these terms are borrowed from industrial labor relations.

The public is compared to the stockholders of a private corporation. A 1969 report by the Maritime Trades Department of the AFL-CIO, entitled "Collective Bargaining in the Public Sector," contained this passage:

> The public considers its stake more directly involved with public employees than with private employees, and strikes and work stoppages, therefore, are against

the public as a whole. Some argue that any attempts to organize or join a union or bargain in any way are not in the "public interest." This argument of "public interest" is as fallacious as to say that the stockholders are the real employees (*sic*—employers) in the private sector.

Labor leaders are vigorously seeking to equate private and public labor relations and to have the systems of private employment applied to the public sector. Is there no essential difference between a strike by policemen or auto workers, firemen or carpenters, teachers or steelworkers?

In applying itself to these questions, the AFL-CIO report gave this answer:

> Public employees, individually and collectively, are like employees anywhere. Secretaries type letters in the public sector as well as in the private. Men drive trucks, or work at desks or run machines. Their functions for the most part (except for law enforcement officers) are basically the same. The public employee is neither "subversive" nor "anarchistic." His demands —which are long overdue—are merely the natural and healthy consequence of the relationship between labor and management in a free society.
>
> Fifty years ago, when Calvin Coolidge sent his famous telegram denying the right of public employees to strike, the boundaries of the private and public sectors were easily discernible.
>
> Those boundaries no longer clearly exist. They have blurred in the face of overlapping functions, parallel efforts and incredibly complex relationships. This massive erosion has occurred gradually and peacefully.

ARE PUBLIC AND PRIVATE EMPLOYERS THE SAME?

Some public transportation today is publicly owned, as in New York City, some is privately owned, as in Washington, D. C.; public and private schools both serve children in New York as well as in Washington; federal funds underwrite major construction and research programs at leading private universities as well as at public institutions; the railroad industry, privately owned, is very closely linked to the public interest.

Only in one way are the public and private sectors still shackled by an insistence that they be "different."

This is at the bargaining table.

This bitter irony is the cause of the serious protest among public sector employees. There is no valid excuse for denying public employees the same rights that private employees have in a country which has struck down laws denying equal treatment to human beings on the basis of race, creed or religious origins. This equality must apply in labor relations as well, especially when the two sectors perform large portions of identical work. Government cannot continue to legislate for private employees while denying public employees the same protections. Governments seem determined that the proverbial goose and gander not enjoy the same sauce—and for no really legitimate reason. The rights of employees—all employees—must be the same at the bargaining table.

That statement expresses labor's views: Public and private labor are the same and disputes among both must be handled in the same way.

Are they the same?

Many forms of labor are. Typing is typing and bus driving is bus driving, whether performed for a private or public employer. The same statement could be made about thousands of other occupations, from architect to zoologist. But, as pointed out previously, some of the largest groups of public employees have only a small counterpart in the private sector. These include policemen, firemen, sanitation workers, water and sewage employees, and public welfare social workers.

Labor is stating an obvious truth when it points out that many privately employed workers perform more vital functions in an urban society than do many types of public workers. Strikes by employees of electric utilities, railroads, fuel delivery, and food manufacturing companies could have far greater impact on public health and safety than a walkout of municipal clerks. A strike by privately employed school bus drivers can have as debilitating an effect on some school systems as a walkout by teachers.

Yet, are private and public *employers* the same? A private corporation is owned by its stockholders, who have voluntarily invested money in the business by buying shares of its stock. The stockholders—and a large corporation may have millions of them—elect by ballot a board of directors to run the company. The directors generally will be major stockholders, important customers or suppliers of the corporation, experts in its particular fields, and prominent citizens. The board of directors elects a chairman who becomes the chief executive officer of the corporation, and other officers such as president, vice-presidents, secretary, treasurer, and legal counsel. The officers and the people they select to assist them are called "management."

The stockholders of the company, through a method of indirect representation, have selected people to operate the company as efficiently as possible. If the company is not operated successfully, stockholders have the power to re-

Transportation strikes by both public and private workers have the same effect on travelers. The congestion above was caused by commuters jamming into Grand Central Station during the 1966 public transit strike in New York City. Below, New Jersey commuters wait for buses during a train strike by private employees in 1970.

place the directors and management. This has occurred many times.

There is somewhat of a parallel in the American system of government. In some local governments, voters elect a council or board of commissioners that selects a chief executive from among its members. At the national, state, and most municipal levels, voters elect both a legislative body (Congress, legislature, or council) and the chief executive (president, governor, or mayor). Other leading officials are either elected, as in most states, or appointed, as at the federal level (the Cabinet), with the advice and consent of the legislative body.

If someone, such as a labor leader, were trying to equate private and public management, he could argue that the differences between corporate and governmental structure are procedural and minor.

The analogy breaks down, however, when the *powers* of corporate versus governmental management are considered. A corporation manufactures a product or performs a service that it sells to customers with the object of making a profit. It has free choice in selecting the products or services in which it deals. It can add new ones at will or discontinue old ones. It must make a profit, although it can function if it breaks even or possibly loses money for short periods of time. In determining the division of the profits, the corporate directors are free to decide how much money is to be either reinvested in the business, conserved for future use, or divided among the stockholders.

Governments do not ordinarily manufacture products. Only a handful of governments operate electric utilities. A few products are sold, such as residue from sewage plants for fertilizer. But these are all minor, ancillary operations. The main "business" of government is to provide

ARE PUBLIC AND PRIVATE EMPLOYERS THE SAME?

services, police and fire protection, sanitation, water, sewage, public education, and the rest. Government is run on a nonprofit basis—it is not in business to make money. Only rarely does a government have a surplus of revenues over expenditures, and then no attempt is made to divide this among taxpayers. At the same time, governments can "lose" money only with difficulty. The national government has for years engaged in deficit financing, that is, spending more than its revenues and borrowing money to make up the difference. Most state and local governments do not engage in this practice. It is frequently forbidden by law. Both corporations and governments can borrow money from banks or raise money through the sale of bonds for long-term investments in buildings, equipment, highways, bridges, and other major projects.

A private corporation has nearly free choice in deciding what it will charge for its products or services. The only restrictions are in those industries regulated by government, such as public utilities, railroads, and other transportation companies. Most private companies also have a self-imposed restriction—competition. The amounts they charge must be approximately equal to those of rival firms.

In only a few instances do governments charge for their services. There are often charges for water and sewage services, refuse collection, and use of transit, postal, library, meeting rooms, and a few other facilities. These charges are calculated to be minimal. At best they are intended to make the service self-supporting, but usually they defray only part of the operational expenses. In only the rarest instances does a government make a profit on a service. The great bulk of governmental operations, which carry no charge with them, include police and fire protection, public education, street maintenance, welfare, and inspection of buildings and products—the list is very long.

While a government is overwhelmingly dependent upon taxes for its revenues, it is not free to determine the amount they will be. The process of taxation is rigidly controlled by law. Public officials simply cannot increase taxation at will. Every tax and most charges must be voted by the elected representatives of the people and often by the people themselves.

If a private corporation wishes or is forced by a strike to pay its employees more money, it has several options. It can reduce its profits, increase the charges for its products and services, launch a campaign to increase its sales and thus its revenues, reduce expenditures by cutting production, install automated equipment to lessen the need for manpower, or dispense with certain products or services. It can even go out of business altogether and divide the assets among the stockholders. Or, the business can be sold to another corporation.

In a similar situation a government has considerably fewer options. It has no profits to reduce in size. In only a few instances can it increase charges for its services. It can increase revenues from existing sources only when economic prosperity raises private earnings and expenditures. It can in some cases install automated equipment to lessen the need for manpower, but it cannot usually reduce the amount of its services and only rarely can it dispense with a service. Government cannot go out of business. The closest parallel is for a city, for example, to turn over a service to the state. Above all, a government, unlike a private corporation, cannot move to a new location where the cost of doing business is lower.

Only on a temporary basis can government raise money by reducing one service to pay the increased cost of

ARE PUBLIC AND PRIVATE EMPLOYERS THE SAME?

another. In a given year it can apply a "job freeze," that is, refuse to hire or replace workers. But this cannot go on for long. Except for the federal government, which can go into debt, most state and local governments must increase taxes to pay wage increases.

Can a tax increase be compared to a raise in prices? It is easy for a corporation to increase its prices. The corporation simply says, "we are raising our prices." But such decisions are usually rather agonized. The corporate management fears it will lose business to competitors or that consumers will refuse to use the higher priced product.

But the difficulty a corporation has in raising prices bears no comparison to the problem government officials face in increasing taxes. There is, as noted, the legal process of raising taxes. Of far greater importance is politics. Public officials are elected every few years by the taxpayers, and the amount of taxation is of primary concern to voters. It is axiomatic in politics that taxes are never raised in an election year. In fact, to raise taxes at any time can be an invitation to political defeat, for although the public must pay the increase and cannot use a competitor's products as in the case of the private corporation, they need not reelect the officials who are raising the taxes. There is only the remotest parallel between politics in the private and public sectors.

For all these reasons it is farfetched to equate private and public employers, even those that employ many of the same type of workers. The crux of the matter is the crucial role of the taxpayer in government. He cannot be compared to either the stockholders or the customers of a corporation. In a word, public and private labor are not in the same position.

But are labor leaders correct when they say that private

and public labor can be *treated* the same? Can the methods used to settle labor disputes in the private sector be used in the public sector? This is a question that requires careful examination, for unions state emphatically that these methods are not only the best, but perhaps the only ones that will solve public labor disputes.

CHAPTER 8

Can Collective Bargaining Prevent Public Strikes?

THE LONG HISTORY of labor turmoil in the United States predates the founding of the Republic. For the last century and longer, labor disputes were marked with violence, bloodshed, human suffering and economic chaos. Gradually, largely through trial and error and with a measure of government legislation, industry and labor worked out a system to minimize, although not eliminate, strikes and other forms of labor strife.

The system in use today is a partnership between labor, industry, and government. A series of laws passed in the 1930's and 1940's established the rights and responsibilities of labor and management and created government machinery to ensure both.

Workers now have the right to organize into unions, and those unions have the right to represent their workers in negotiations with employers. If two or more unions are competing for the right to represent workers, the National Labor Relations Board holds an election among the workers. The union that wins the election has the exclusive right to represent the workers in question. This procedure seems very routine today, but when it was passed in the 1930's it was a most progressive piece of legislation. It prevented a company from establishing a "friendly" union with which it could negotiate more easily.

Members of each union govern their own affairs. They elect officers, adopt a constitution, hold a national convention, and vote on policies affecting the union. The officers of a labor union are thus as much "political animals" as are public officials. They hold office at the discretion of the voting members. If those officers fail to please the membership, they can be voted out of office.

In the private sector, workers have a positive right to strike. If a strike imperils national safety and health, the government can require the strikers to return to work for an eighty-day "cooling off" period, during which the strike will hopefully be settled. If it is not, the workers can then strike. Workers have a legal right to remain off the job as long as they feel necessary and to picket the company property in an orderly, peaceful manner. They are forbidden by law to engage in such "unfair labor practices" as a sit-down strike or a secondary boycott. In a sit-down, the workers refuse to leave the company property. In a secondary boycott they picket companies doing business with the strikebound plant. In the view of the law, the strike must be directed against the particular company employing the workers and no one else.

Employers are also legally bound to permit the workers to strike without interference. They cannot "lock out" workers, that is, refuse to admit workers who wish to work. For example, during negotiations a company cannot refuse to admit workers as a means of forcing the union into a

New York sanitation workers in the 1940's picket for fair union representation.

settlement. Likewise, companies cannot fire strikers and hire "scabs," or strikebreakers, to replace them.

The aim of these and numerous other regulations is to force union and management to compromise and come to terms. In actual practice, employees work under a contract negotiated with the company. The contract spells out in detail all the terms of employment, fringe benefits, working conditions, and the rights and responsibilities of each party. The contract invariably contains a no-strike pledge; that is, the union agrees not to strike during the term of the contract, which may be one or more years.

The government tries to assist labor and management in settling labor disputes. The Federal Mediation and Conciliation Service provides experienced men to help resolve the deadlock. The mediators normally talk to each side separately to learn the issues at stake. They then bring the two sides together in a mood of cooperation, and suggestions are made for possible settlements. The government also provides "fact finding" services. When the facts of a dispute are a subject of disagreement, impartial persons determine the true facts. Arbitration is also available when both sides agree to call in impartial persons to decide the issue. The arbitrators' findings may be "advisory" to be used in reaching a negotiated settlement. Or the parties may agree in advance that the arbitration is "binding"; that is, both sides will accept the arbitrators' findings, whatever they may be.

Two procedures are of paramount importance in maintaining labor peace in the private sector. One is the grievance procedure, which is included in every wage contract. A grievance is basically a complaint by a worker or group of workers that they are being treated unfairly or that the wage contract is being violated. The grievance machinery is aimed at preventing the complaints from building into

Mayor John Lindsay (left) confers with the mediation panel attempting to settle New York City's 1966 transit strike. Before an agreement can be reached, the mediators meet separately with each side.

major dissatisfactions that could lead to wildcat strikes. The grievance procedures generally call for conferences between management and labor officials at various levels, and an impasse is usually settled by binding arbitration. Grievance procedures are generally unknown to the public, yet they are the lifeblood of labor-management relations.

The second procedure is collective bargaining. Labor and management sit down as equals and bargain over wages, working conditions, and whatever else is an issue. The union makes a demand; the company replies with an offer. The union presents facts and arguments to support its demands; management defends its position in a similar fashion.

Traditionally, the demand and the offer are far apart—and deliberately so. Both union and management know they will compromise, meet somewhere in the middle. The aim is to move the "middle" closer to one side or the other. There is normally a great deal of give-and-take. The union may offer to accept greater retirement, health, and other fringe benefits in place of wages, or management may make such an offer. The company may demand greater productivity from workers to offset the wage demands. A host of ways can be found to narrow the differences, but the services of a mediator may be needed. Eventually an agreement is reached, and a wage contract is drawn up and signed amid mutual smiles and congratulations. In recent years about 90 percent of all labor disputes have been settled through collective bargaining, rather than by a strike.

If the grievance procedure is the lifeblood of labor-management relations, collective bargaining is the heart and soul. The two sides meet as adversaries, each determined to get as much as possible or to give as little as possible. Bargaining may be tough and hard. But the aim is to reach some sort of agreement short of a strike. Both sides keep themselves prepared for collective bargaining. Corporations employ a full-time staff of people who are experts in labor relations and do nothing but work in this field. Labor unions likewise work full time at representing workers.

One other feature of collective bargaining is important. Negotiations take place in secret. Results are announced, but the negotiators do not have their words monitored by either union members or superiors of the management negotiators. A freer give-and-take results.

When a strike occurs in private industry today it is generally over some "gut" issue and is frequently predictable in advance. The two sides are so far apart in their demands and offers and are so adamant in not giving in that there is no chance for settlement. The issue in the 1970 General Motors strike, for example, was the insistence of workers on increased wages to offset the high cost of living in the United States, as well as to improve their retirement system. In opposition, the corporation felt that higher wages would mean increased car prices, further damaging the ability of American cars to compete with low-priced foreign imports. With both sides feeling they were right, both marshaling facts and statistics to support their positions, the strike was inevitable.

Organized labor wants to apply the same methods used in the private sector to the resolution of public labor disputes. It wants the right to organize workers into a union and to represent those workers in negotiations with government officials. It wants a system created for determining exclusive union representation. It wants a grievance procedure, collective bargaining, and the right to strike.

A significant amount of the labor strife in the public sector has resulted from the efforts of workers and unions to achieve these goals. Government officials have refused to recognize unions or to negotiate with them, and strikes have resulted. One study estimates that 27 percent of the public work stoppages have been caused by failure to recognize unions and to meet with them in good faith.

Labor leaders point out that strife has been minimal in those places where there is a mechanism for union recognition and collective bargaining, notably Wisconsin and Connecticut.

Nevertheless, some problems occur when government seeks to adopt private industry's methods of achieving labor peace. Foremost among the problems is the right to strike.

In labor's long experience in private industry, the right to strike is absolutely essential. Management knows that the workers will strike if an agreement is not reached, and this threat lends an earnestness to the negotiations. The expiration date of the existing wage contract is normally the deadline for negotiations. If an agreement is not reached there will be a strike. Labor leaders usually enter the negotiations bearing the permission of union members to call a strike whenever they wish. Labor leaders have often stated that collective bargaining is meaningless without the right to strike. Labor contends that management will not bargain seriously if they know in advance that the workers will not or cannot strike.

For this reason alone, labor leaders insist the no-strike laws for public employees must go. They point out that nearly all labor disputes in the private sector are resolved through collective bargaining. And they insist that the same can be done in the public sector, if union officials could only enter negotiations with the ultimate weapon—the strike.

Union officials have said repeatedly that no one wants

to strike. A most effective statement of this stand was made by Jerry Wurf, president of the American Federation of State, County, and Municipal Employees.

> Nobody ever prints this but I say it to our staff and I say it to our membership. I am opposed to strikes. I don't want strikes. They're bad. They're hard on the city but they're harder on the workers. I fight bitterly for the right to strike—the *right* to strike. But I don't think there's any principle involved in striking. Striking is a tactic to persuade an employer to deal with us. If it can be avoided, almost any price ought to be paid in order to avoid a strike.

Based upon its long experience in private industry, labor is saying that without the right to strike, labor enters collective bargaining in an inferior position. If management knows that the workers will not or cannot strike, it is much less apt to bargain in good faith.

But the situation between private industry and government is not analogous. Private industry management can decide that the issues at stake are of such importance that it will permit a strike to occur, sometimes for a very long time, to force the workers to accept less than their original demands. In effect, industry management says: This issue is of crucial importance to us. We are willing to permit the strike and lose a great deal of earnings and profits to win our point. There are even instances of companies going out of business entirely rather than giving in to wage demands. A famous instance was the Brooklyn *Eagle* newspaper, which stopped publication in 1955.

Can a government make this decision? It cannot go out of business, certainly. In many cases it cannot permit a strike. It cannot allow strikes by policemen and firemen.

Indeed, most labor officials, including Wurf, admit that these two categories of public employees cannot strike. But there are other categories of workers who also create public hardship by striking, including transit, sanitation, welfare, and postal employees. Thus, government officials cannot permit certain types of strikes to occur at all, and others must be kept to a very short duration.

The question to be asked is this: If unions have the right to strike, does that not tip the scales and put public officials in an inferior position at the bargaining table? They cannot permit certain types of strikes, therefore in bargaining they must capitulate to union demands, find the money someplace, and, eventually, face the voters' wrath when taxes are raised.

It is an impasse. The right to strike makes government inferior; the absence of it puts unions in the inferior position.

Another problem in transferring collective bargaining to the public sector is politics. In private industry, management must pay close attention to profit and loss, sales, product quality, and many other things, but politics in the sense of holding on to their jobs is a minor consideration. James Roche, the head of General Motors, does not have to engage in anything remotely resembling a popularity contest among the corporate stockholders. He does not have to kiss babies, shake hands, and otherwise ingratiate himself among the stockholders while demonstrating that he is a capable leader and an efficient administrator who keeps taxes at a minimum. He can, of course, be replaced, but the situation is only remotely analogous to that of a mayor, governor, or president, who must go to the voters at regular intervals, maintain his popularity, and establish his ability to govern.

Politics constantly enters into collective bargaining in

Police and firemen in Youngstown, Ohio, on strike in 1967 after negotiations between the city and the workers fail to bring about a settlement.

the public sector. The voter looks over the shoulders of both public officials and the union representatives. Consider only two of the work stoppages described in Chapter 5. The union leaders in San Francisco made every effort to settle the strike because they did not wish to damage politically a mayor who was popular with them. In the Cleveland strike, union officials admitted they did not want to cause the defeat of a black mayor. It is at least conceivable that union leaders might be tempted to embarrass a government official whom they did not like or support politically. What better way than by striking?

Another problem: The chief management negotiator in private industry customarily has high rank in the corporation. Commonly he is a vice-president of the company, with a direct line of communication to the board of directors and its chairman. If the negotiator feels he can reach a settlement of the dispute by granting a certain amount of dollars in pay raises, he can get immediate approval or disapproval. A mayor or governor or president usually cannot do this. Under the American system of tripartite government, pay raises often have to be approved by city councils, legislatures, or Congress. And, such legislative bodies frequently have minds of their own. It is not unusual for them to be in competition politically with the chief executive. This, as we have seen, was a major factor in the postal strike. In short, government negotiators do not always have the same freedom in decision-making as private negotiators. Government processes are simply more cumbersome.

Still another difficulty: Union officials, particularly those affiliated with the AFL-CIO, have had long experience in labor relations in the private sector. They have been working at this task for decades. Government officials, except in the most unusual circumstances, simply have had less experience and are less aware of the intricacies of labor relations. Thus, they are at a disadvantage.

Some of the intricacies of labor-management relations were spelled out by C. T. Spivey, vice-president in charge of labor relations for the United States Steel Corporation, in an address to the Federal Management Improvement Conference in Washington, D. C., in September, 1970. Spivey noted:

> Students of labor relations have frequently observed that the most stable labor situation exists where there is a strong and responsible union on the one hand and a similarly strong, responsible employer on the other. . . . I would say that we have our best labor relations where there are competent, honest representatives on both sides who have not only the authority, but the strength to make the decisions required of them. And, I might also add, where there is some degree of mutual respect between them.

He said the "prime importance" of competent personnel in labor relations was "obvious."

> Thus, if I had to recommend one element above all others for attention, it would be this matter of the selection and development of able labor relations representatives. To my way of thinking, it really boils down to this—this two-way labor relations street is a tough and precarious road, but it can work, and work well, with the right people; with the wrong people, it will work only with the greatest difficulty, and maybe not at all.

Spivey described United States Steel's program for developing its labor representatives. They must be interested in the work and they must have experience among the workers themselves. Then the company spends a great deal of money and effort in educating and training them.

Spivey placed great importance upon the language of the written agreement and said that disputes "stemming from hastily conceived or poorly written language" tend to be of a "particularly nasty" variety. He said the grievance procedures were of utmost importance in industrial labor relations, but emphasized the usefulness of informal meetings between union officials and management to air complaints and come to a meeting of minds about mutual problems.

Contrast was provided by Kenneth Moffett of the Federal Mediation and Conciliation Service, which has mediated many public labor disputes. He said one difference between the private and public sector "is the lack of experience or sophistication on the part of the representatives of the parties. Collective bargaining in the public sector is relatively new and, while there are knowledgeable practitioners in the field, these are relatively few."

He described a dispute in which a football coach was the government's chief negotiator in a school dispute.

> While no offense is meant to football coaches, it is most unlikely that such individuals have the training and experience required to handle bargaining matters. The lack of experience can result in the creation of unnecessary issues which serve to impede the discussion process and hamper the resolution of basic disputes.

Another example involved a negotiating session between striking city social workers and "city fathers." A federal mediator was called into the session.

CAN COLLECTIVE BARGAINING PREVENT STRIKES?

In the room with him were the city council, the invited public, the press and the live microphone of a local radio station. Understandably the result of the first day's negotiations was no progress. Both sides were talking for the record and to the public—they were making speeches, not negotiating. It was not until subsequent negotiations were held behind closed doors that progress and an eventual settlement were made.

Among the glaring faults, in addition to the inexperience of bargainers, were failures to give negotiators authority to make agreements and failure to set a deadline for the end of negotiations. As to the latter, Moffett said:

To overcome this handicap, the service has been forced to create pressures on the parties to keep them bargaining. Such was the situation where the mediator found the parties had been bargaining for many months without progress. To stimulate movement, the mediator set a reasonable time limit for his availability, thus creating a sense of urgency. As a result of his imposing such a restriction, the agreement was reached within the time limits he created.

Another view of the problems of inexperienced public negotiators was expressed by Sam Zagoria, director of the Labor-Management Relations Service.

I have been told that fully half of the mayors in city halls this year [1970] are in their first term, and some are forced to learn the hard realities of employer-employee relations in overnight instant education. Employee tensions, some frustrated and built up by months of official avoidance, will not always await proper on-the-job education of public employers in the philosophy and practice of collective negotiations.

He said some government leaders, relying on no-strike laws and long periods of uninterrupted service by workers, have given low priority to labor relations.

> True, the presence of legal prohibitions and penalties is a deterrent to many more stoppages, but the mayor who thinks "it can't happen here" may some day face a "happening" on his doorstep and it may not be a birthday party. . . .
> Faced with this new potent factor in employee relations, communities have reacted in various ways, and in the opinion of some, overreacted occasionally, too. A few have treated a union as a foreign invader, trespassing on sovereign soil, and learned to their dismay the wisdom of a former vice president of the national Association of Manufacturers, Charles Kothe, who declared that unions are organized from the inside, not the outside. Other communities have swung to the other extreme, hastening to recognize and agree to the broadest demands of the union. This is not to say that a city should stand like a stone wall in exacting unreasonable terms and conditions any more than a union should have free play in writing a first contract.

He said cities are "handicapped by their lack of preparation" for labor negotiations.

> Union officials are usually primed for the execution of recognition agreements and the negotiation of labor contracts, but local government officials are rarely ready. A result, occasionally, is recognition of a bar-

gaining unit and adoption of an agreement which represents more a straitjacket than a tailor-made document covering a fair and workable resolution of labor-management problems. Such provisions may be years in altering.

Among the mistakes made by public officials is the fragmentation of bargaining units through union recognition. In New York City, 90 unions and other employee organizations negotiate for 200 separate contracts. Detroit has 146 bargaining units for 26,000 employees. Milwaukee even conducts bargaining with a union consisting of one man.

Such mistakes can prove costly and time consuming to cities, even when a labor relations bureau has been created and staffed with knowledgeable, experienced people. For an elected mayor to enter into such bargaining, as well as carry out his other responsibilities, is hardly likely to contribute to labor peace.

There is one more major problem involved in transferring private sector labor relations techniques to government—the role of the public in government. The most highly competent government and union representatives might seat themselves at a bargaining table and work out an ideal agreement that resolves a labor dispute, but if the public does not want it or accept it, then the agreement is meaningless. The public has the power to express that disagreement—at the polls, by mail, mass meetings, and other forms of protest. A labor union willing to strike what it conceives as "public management" of a city or state government might well have second thoughts about striking a determined public that was in opposition to them.

Eventually, both public officials and labor will have to carry on public education campaigns to convince the voters of the need for and wisdom of the negotiated agreements. In the private sector, labor unions attempt to engage public sympathy for their position. But the task may be considerably intensified when the public is being greatly inconvenienced by the strike and being asked to pay higher taxes at the same time.

For all these reasons, there are serious problems involved in transferring private techniques of labor relations to government. These difficulties are the root of the various other proposals for different techniques, such as "meet and confer" and "required to negotiate" laws, as well as the no-strike laws. At the same time, labor is insisting upon collective bargaining and the right to strike as essential to labor peace. Strikes have occurred in an effort to obtain these prerogatives.

To avoid the impasse and the resultant labor strife, responsible individuals among both government officials and labor are experimenting with a whole new approach to labor relations in the public sector.

CHAPTER 9

The Search
for a Better Way

THE TWO TOP officials in the federal government in the field of employee relations addressed the convention of the American Federation of Government Employees, AFL-CIO, in Denver in August, 1970. Their remarks illustrated a new government attitude toward employees and the search for a new way to solve labor disputes.

W. J. Usery, Jr., assistant secretary of labor, sought to illustrate the new government attitude toward labor problems in the wake of the postal strike.

> I think it is safe to say that 200,000 postal employees on strike at major centers of the United States poses the need for some new thinking.
>
> It reminded me of the man who crossed a parakeet with a tiger.
>
> When they asked him what he got, he replied, "I don't know what it is, but when it speaks, I listen."
>
> Well, we found ourselves with a postal employee

who had been crossed with a picket line. We were not sure what we had, but you can believe it spoke loud and clear and we heard it!

The second official was Robert E. Hampton, chairman of the United States Civil Service Commission.

> ... many suggestions were made to superimpose on the Federal system the private sector industrial patterns. . . . I personally reject this imposition. No system, public or private, can or should be devised with the aim of avoiding conflict. Conflict is inevitable if problems are to be faced rather than swept under the rug. This does not mean, however, that an adversary situation, as is often the case in private industry, should be permitted in the federal government.
> To the contrary, we have an opportunity to build a new system, a better system, geared to avoiding polarization of the parties and treating conflict as a source of creative thinking and resolution. At the same time, we have the opportunity to draw upon the many years of experience in the private sector and extract from that system those elements which work best and which are adaptable to the public service environment. . . .
> It is quite clear to me that we have a real opportunity to pioneer a better system of dealing with the problems of public service unionism if we can deal with each other openly and with candor. . . .
> If we can concentrate on our mutual goals and problems and tackle our differences openly, intelligently and properly we will avoid the clashes of muscle and power which have marked labor-management relations at other levels of public employment and in

the private sector. We're big enough to work out our own system together rather than adopting in toto another system not designed for our needs or our time.

The federal government is listening to workers and unions, and it is trying to work out a new system for handling labor disputes. As Hampton expressed it, government will borrow some of the practices from the private sector, but the heart of the new system ought to be cooperation rather than antagonism in labor relations.

History would seem to support this view. Industrial labor-management techniques were developed in the 1930's, after a century of violence and antipathy—and then only after Congress enacted laws protecting unions and their right to strike and bargain with employers. Public workers, despite the spate of recent strikes, do not have this long history of antagonism. Public employees and elected officials generally worked well together until just a few years ago. This split resulted in official neglect of worker complaints, but if the neglect has ended then there is reason to hope, at least, that the aura of cooperation that used to exist can return to government service.

Furthermore, the situation that tends to cause antagonism in industry does not exist in government. In industry, management represents the stockholders, and the object of management is to make as high a profit as possible for them. Top managers of corporations usually receive extremely high salaries, in some cases hundreds of thousands of dollars a year. The workers are employed on behalf of the stockholders. It is natural, probably inevitable, that workers should demand a larger share of the company profits.

The situation in government is radically different. There is no profit to be shared by anyone. Both elected officials and the workers are employed by the public—and both are members of the public. For workers and officials to view each other as adversaries and attempt to get the most they can out of the other, as often happens in private industry, is to create an artificial situation that can only be described as nonsensical. To repeat for emphasis: There is no one in private sector labor relations whose role is the same as that of the public in government labor relations.

The origins of the federal government's efforts to find a better way to handle labor problems was President Kennedy's executive order in 1962. It permitted union recognition and limited collective bargaining. In 1967, President Johnson appointed a Task Force on Employee-Management Relations to look into the way in which President Kennedy's order was being administered and to recommend methods to improve its effectiveness. The task force, chaired by Labor Secretary Willard Wirtz, made a thorough study and recommended many changes. The White House, however, never released their report to the public. Instead it was published as an addendum to the Labor Department's annual report on the eve of the Johnson administration's departure from Washington. The White House failed to accept the report apparently because the secretary of defense believed the report's recommendations would conflict with the secretary's authority to manage his agency.

Substantial portions of the Wirtz report were included in Executive Order 11491, entitled Labor-Management Relations in the Federal Service, which was signed by President Nixon on October 29, 1969. It went into effect on January 1, 1970. The major provisions of the order are as follows:

- It establishes the Federal Labor Relations Council

as a central authority to administer and interpret the order. The council is composed of the chairman of the Civil Service Commission, the Secretary of Labor, and an official of the Office of Management and Budget, which is part of the White House.

• The assistant secretary of labor for labor-management relations is given authority to decide representation and unfair labor practices cases. Thus, the assistant secretary will perform singlehandedly many of the functions of the National Labor Relations Board in the private sector.

• Third-party procedures are set up for resolving bargaining impasses. The third-party functions are to be provided by the Federal Mediation and Conciliation Service and the newly created Federal Service Impasses Panel. The panel, consisting of three or more members appointed by the president, has authority to direct fact finding or arbitration and can take any action necessary to resolve impasses.

• The order clarifies and broadens the scope of negotiations. A union may appeal the question of negotiability to the Federal Labor Relations Council. A federal agency can disapprove a negotiated agreement only when it conflicts with the law, published policy, or regulations of appropriate authorities outside the agency.

• The principle of exclusive union recognition is embraced. Secret ballot elections, supervised by the assistant secretary of labor, are required to determine exclusive recognition.

• Supervisors are not included in the order. Rather a system of consultation is established to deal with complaints of supervisors.

• The order permits binding arbitration of grievances and disputes over interpretation and application of negotiated agreements.

- The union shop, agency shop, and other types of union security measures, except for the voluntary dues checkoff, are forbidden. (A union shop is one where employees are required to join a union; in an agency shop, the union acts as an agent and collects dues from all employees, whether or not they are union members.) The order protects the right of workers either to join or not join a union.
- Public unions are required to report their financial data and permit democratic procedures in governing the union, as in the private sector.

Reaction to the order has been less than enthusiastic. Government officials feel it is possibly a "first step" or "progress." A variety of union officials have denounced it. Perhaps the biggest criticism of the new system lies in the fact that the postal strike and air controllers' sick-out occurred months after the order was in effect.

There is, in all candor, a quality of desperation in the statements of leading government officials in behalf of the order. It is not an exaggeration to say that officials are begging unions to give the machinery of the order a chance to operate and not insist upon the collective bargaining techniques of private industry.

Hampton, in the speech quoted earlier, said:

> While there has not been . . . total agreement with the order's provisions, we must agree the new Executive Order represents significant improvement over the old. . . .

He said unions and management must "redouble" their

efforts to work out a sound labor relations policy. Management must avoid neglecting labor problems until they lead to a strike. Unions must give government time.

As an aftermath of the strikes, there were those who said, before the ink was dry, the Executive Order was out of date; and there were those who said we must adopt the policy of "full collective bargaining" from the private sector, with all the rituals, trappings and adversary conditions that it implies. We disagree. Government management is not ready for full collective bargaining and neither are the unions. Until Congress gives the executive branch the full economic package (to set wages, for example), it would be impossible anyway. In the future maybe—today it could not be done.

Similar comments came from Tony Ingrassia, director of the Office of Labor-Management Relations of the United States Civil Service Commission. He said, in an address to a government labor organization, "I know you are not happy with all provisions of the Order." Then he listed what he considered the "principal gains for unions" in the new program. Among those were the establishment of a central authority to handle negotiations, the use of third parties to settle disputes, the requirement of good faith bargaining, improved techniques for union recognition, and more accurate definitions of negotiable matters. In another speech, Ingrassia called the present labor-management situation in the federal government "spring training" for future relations. He said labor could spend all its time denouncing the order, but urged them to devote the time to finding out how to make it work.

The biggest difficulty with the order is that it still calls for only limited collective bargaining. Ingrassia admitted this:

> Since negotiable matters are limited to those matters within the authority of the agency head, it is basically accurate to say that only about 25 per cent of those matters of interest to employees and their union representatives are covered by the order, specifically those personnel policies, practices and matters affecting working conditions within the agency head's authority.

Ingrassia said this was not a "small area by any means," and could cover as many as 265 items "ranging from advance sick leave and grievance arbitration to wash up time and work measurement—from A to W if not A to Z." He added, however:

> It is true, nevertheless, that about 50 per cent . . . of those matters employees and unions are primarily interested in are determined by Congress, through legislation. For example, salaries, health insurance and life insurance premiums, annual leave and sick leave. The remaining 25 per cent are those personnel policies transcending one-agency application, primarily determined by the Civil Service Commission under legal authority and direction.

The most important monetary issues are not subject to collective bargaining. It must be said that President Nixon did not have the power to make money a bargainable issue, if he had wanted to. Wages, insurance, retirement, and other such matters are decided by Congress.

Yet, as the postal strike proved, militant workers can

make money a matter for collective bargaining, whether it is supposed to be or not. Usery described what happened:

> The catalyst which precipitated these new developments [in government labor relations] was, of course, the strike of the postal workers earlier this year. It was a historic event. It did not come about without warning. It was just that nobody seemed to believe it would ever really happen.
>
> When the government moved to respond to that situation, I found myself taking part in the strangest kind of collective bargaining that any of us in the public sector had ever before encountered.
>
> None of us at the sessions in Washington had, under existing law, any authority or official status in these negotiations. The Postmaster General, the representatives of the seven postal unions holding exclusive recognition at the national level, Jim Gildea of the AFL-CIO, acting as spokesman for the unions, and I, as a mediator, were bargaining over postal employees' pay. Congress alone could decide the questions we were trying to find the answers to.
>
> But if we were in a unique position in these discussions, then it is because we—and I mean we, as a nation—were faced with a unique situation which called for invention and new responses.

The postal strike proved to millions of government workers that in a strike government officials are forced to bargain over wages, whether they want to or not and whether it is legal or not.

An effort is underway to transfer power over federal wages from Congress to the executive branch, presumably after collective bargaining takes place. Most observers feel it is rather unlikely that Congress will surrender its prerogatives very quickly, if ever.

Even the collective bargaining that does exist under the Nixon order has been criticized by union executives. David Silvergleid, president of the National Postal Union, third largest union of postal employees, has criticized both the order and the settlement reached after the postal strike. Many of his comments pertain to the government's system for granting exclusive representation rights to unions. He maintains the government has elected to recognize craft unions and ignore industry-wide unions such as the National Postal Union. Aside from these jurisdictional disputes within labor, Silvergleid made these other criticisms:

> No matter how sliced, management alone will determine the appropriate bargaining unit under . . . [the order], since it alone has the power to determine the kind of unit that will promote efficiency. You may rest assured that it will make determinations that are in its interests. History has already shown that management in the public sector acts in much the same way as in the private.

He criticized the makeup of the Federal Labor Relations Council.

> Put bluntly, management will decide for itself what is good for federal employees. The architects of . . . [the order] still dream of federal company unions, but they dream in vain. Under the order, management's single greatest power appears to lie in its right to determine the nature of its bargaining adversary. The order makes it clear that where management

establishes a national unit tailored to its liking, "no recognition shall be granted to any other labor organization for employees within the national exclusive unit". . . .

Much else is wrong with the order. Not the least is the unfair labor practice procedure which places the final decision with management—the Assistant Secretary of Labor. Such is the order that no agreement negotiated by a union with management is binding unless approved by the head of the Agency concerned. How good-faith bargaining can take place under such an arrangement is beyond this observer.

Deadlocks in negotiations will, under the order, go to a Federal Service Impasses Panel which will be named by the President and which will decide how the impasse shall be settled. Put bluntly, management will have the final voice and, of course, "father knows best" in all cases. Neither the right to strike nor final and binding arbitration are provided.

Clearly, the era of cooperation sought by federal officials has not yet arrived, at least insofar as Silvergleid is concerned. Nonetheless, it is equally clear that the federal government is determined to seek cooperation with employee unions by discussing mutual problems to find possible solutions. Many federal officials have expressed this, including Usery:

> "Give-and-take" is the name of today's federal labor-management relations game. The flat answer, with the "or else" attached to it, has lost its standing under the new order. . . . I know that federal managers, on the one hand, and government employees and unions

on the other hand, are becoming aware quickly of the need for adjustment. The need, really, for learning how to behave. . . .

I have always found that justice and dignity have an irresistible way of coming to the top. Nothing helps speed their accomplishment more than good will and understanding in our day-to-day work and relationships.

The search for a better solution to public sector labor problems is hardly limited to federal officials. Governors, mayors, and county officials are grappling with these problems as well.

A main thrust of their efforts is to create the machinery for labor relations. State after state, city after city is establishing employee relations bureaus and recruiting or training personnel to staff them. In fact, labor relations in the public sector offers new careers for young people. There is a shortage of trained people. The staff of the employee relations bureau is expected to work full time at improving labor relations and solving labor disputes through consultations, negotiations, or collective bargaining.

The public sector labor experts are using an arsenal of weapons in an effort to avoid strikes. Most involve some form of "third party" intervention, such as mediation, fact finding, and "impasse panels" to develop solutions fair to all, and arbitration both of the advisory and binding variety.

Perhaps the most successful has been New York City's Office of Collective Bargaining, headed by Arvid Anderson. The city government has three hundred thousand employees. It is the largest employer in the city and second in size only to the federal government as a civil service employer. In its 1969 report, the office cited the variety of employees it deals with.

Besides tugboats, the city has been sailing policeboats, fireboats and ferryboats. It runs hospitals, schools, zoos, museums, cafeterias, jails, motor vehicle shops and a radio station. It maintains bridges, parks, high rise apartment houses and office buildings. It polices 6,000 miles of streets and 600 miles of waterfront. It protects 800,000 buildings from fire and theft. It sponsors television programs, live theater, and puppet shows. In all there are at least 800 job titles in city service combined into more than 200 bargaining units represented by scores of employee organizations.

To maintain labor peace in 1969, the Disputes Division of the Office of Collective Bargaining handled twenty-one mediation cases, convened thirty-four impasse panels and processed eighty-five arbitration cases. Anderson added:

Of course, many more situations were resolved without ever having to come before the OCB. In total, 135 contracts involving more than 150,000 employees were negotiated by the Office of Labor Relations and the union, and hundreds of grievances were resolved short of arbitration.

It is a record in which New Yorkers can take justifiable pride.

Whether the New York solution is the best and whether it can be transferred to other localities is open to question. Fact finding, impasse panels, and arbitration have been criticized by both government officials and unions, although both admit they are useful tools in labor disputes. Union leaders dislike binding arbitration because it disrupts the collective bargaining process. They maintain that management will not bargain in good faith if they know the dispute will be settled by arbitrators. The same might also be said of labor negotiators. Government officials dislike arbitration because the arbitrators may be inexpert in city financial problems and legal requirements, and arrive at decisions that are unrealistic in terms of the city's political and financial situation. Detroit in particular has been buffeted by a succession of costly arbitrators' decisions.

The better solution to public sector labor problems has not yet been found, but in many government units it is not for want of trying. The solution being tried most often seems to involve union recognition, creation of expert public employee relations bureaus, some form of negotiation between unions and government officials, and a mixed bag of third-party intervention to resolve impasses.

Two other possible solutions have been suggested by Willoughby Abner, director of the National Center for Dispute Settlement of the American Arbitration Association. He was encountered before as the mediator in the strike in Cleveland, Ohio.

One of Abner's ideas involves a reverse of what now occurs in private industry, wherein government acts as a third-party dispute settler. He suggests that private individuals act as dispute settlers between government officials and public employees. One suggestion is to turn labor problems over to a private, nonprofit agency, such as the National Center. Abner said:

> I just signed an agreement with the Federal Reserve Agency for the National Center to handle the appointments of investigators and hearing officers to investi-

gate unfair labor practice cases that arise within that system. To my knowledge, this is the first time that a federal agency has contracted with a private organization to do this kind of investigative and hearing work on unfair labor practice cases. It is an indication of what I believe must be flexibility and innovation in these areas.

Abner also suggests greater and better use of "joint study committees" in solving public sector labor disputes. He said this approach, unfortunately, was "little used, ill-used and mis-used in the public sector." The sole aim of a joint study committee, composed of both public officials and union representatives, is to study the problems, ascertain the facts, and develop a variety of alternative solutions. The committee report then becomes the basis for collective bargaining or other forms of negotiations. The method short-circuits much of the speechmaking and "grandstanding" in which hard-and-fast demands are issued and refused. The bargaining becomes more rational and aimed more at problem solving. There are fewer places for conventional bargaining tactics intended to best the opponent. The existence of several alternative solutions to the issue reduces the need for desperate, last-minute bargaining to come up with a single solution.

Meanwhile, the search for a better way to solve public labor disputes goes on. The key ingredient being sought is an atmosphere of cooperation rather than antagonism, with the public looking over the participants' shoulders.

CHAPTER 10

A Look at the Future

There is an excellent chance that by 1975 it will cost 25 cents to send a first-class letter within the United States, and that by 1980 it will cost $1.

THOSE WORDS were written by George A. Codding, Jr., professor of political science at the University of Colorado and an expert on the postal system, in the October 5, 1970, issue of *The Nation* magazine. The words are quoted here because they illustrate a fourth possible solution to the problem of labor disputes in the public sector.

Codding based his estimates on two factors. One is that the postal system has long insisted that the first-class mail users pay for the deficits incurred by other classes of mail, especially "junk" mail—the mass of advertisements and circulars that fall like confetti into the nation's mailboxes. In essence the first-class mail users subsidize the junk mail users.

A LOOK AT THE FUTURE

The second factor was the pay increase granted after the postal strike. As Codding expressed it:

> The postman now knows the power of the strike, even one which is not necessarily legal. If the new postal system does not provide him with what he considers a living wage, we may be sure that he will strike again, and again. . . . We shall soon be paying 8 cents for a first-class letter, and according to Postmaster Blount, there will be more to come.

Codding foresaw a result that he did not necessarily decry. He pointed out that the postal system is an "18th century phenomenon, an outgrowth of the discovery of the printing press, the general extension of education, and the expansion of commerce." He went on to write:

> The whole idea of writing out a letter, handing it to someone who carries it across the country or even a town, gives it to its intended recipient who must then open it and read it before he gets the message, is anomalous in the electronic age. It is inefficient and wasteful of time and energy.

He said the postal system has been "kept alive long beyond its time" because it provides mail services to isolated people at reasonable prices, and subsidizes many business enterprises, from the users of junk mail to the railroads, truck, and airline companies that carry the mail.

The nation has far more efficient methods of delivering messages, including telephone, telegraph, teletype, computer print-out, data processing, radio, and television. The newly developed picture phone promises to be a still more efficient way to send messages. As Codding points out, when it cost only a nickel to send a first-class letter, there was no point in even thinking of replacing the postman with an electronic gadget. But at twenty-five cents or fifty cents or a dollar a message, such thoughts take on a measure of practicality. Profit-making communications companies could well go into the business of delivering written messages in competition with the postal system.

Today the postal system is considered indispensable. But if spiraling wage increases led to spiraling postal rate increases—and postage rates are a form of taxation—it is conceivable that ways could and would be found to diminish, or even eliminate, the need for postmen.

There are a number of other "essential" government services that could conceivably become less essential because they cost too much and are inefficient. The mountains of garbage and refuse carried away by sanitation men could be reduced to a molehill. An appliance manufacturer has already marketed a device that crushes large quantities of refuse into a small block of material. Research is in progress to develop easily disintegrated—some have even forecast edible—containers and packages. There may always be a need for a few teachers, but it is at least possible that some of them could be replaced by television sets. The need for policemen could be reduced by commercially manufactured anti-burglary and anti-robbery devices, electronic traffic control devices, and other products. Firemen could be "replaced" by fireproof buildings and automatic fire-dousing equipment installed in buildings. The sick could be treated by automated devices, lessening the need for nurses and hospital aides. If a little imagination is applied, other "indispensable" city services could conceivably be dispensed with.

All of this could be in the category of "blue sky" or "Buck Rogers" fantasies except that there are many examples in the private sector in which spiraling wage increases led to a decline in the use of a product or service.

Until the 1940's, coal was the "indispensable" method of heating the nation's dwellings. When a series of successful strikes by the United Mine Workers raised the price of coal, alternative methods of heating suddenly appeared. The nation underwent a tremendous boom in housing construction following World War II and the most common methods of heating those new homes was by fuel oil and natural gas.

There are many reasons for the decline in the nation's railroad industry, but among them is the high cost of labor, both in wages paid and the low productivity of the workers because of featherbedding or make-work practices. As railroad profits dwindled, service kept pace. Shippers began to use trucks, and travelers turned to cars, buses, and airplanes. The plight of the nation's railroads worsened until Penn Central, the world's largest transportation company, went bankrupt.

A large number of American industries are feeling the pinch of foreign competitors who make cheaper products. To name a few: shipbuilding, textiles, shoes, steel, toys, barber chairs. A principal issue in the General Motors strike was the competition from low-priced European and Japanese cars. The main reason foreign manufacturers can market products at a cheaper price is that both the cost of living and wages are lower. American wages may be the highest in the world, but that is proving to be a mixed blessing.

Thus, there is a fourth possible long-range solution to the problem of labor disputes in the public sector. Rising wages and higher taxation could conceivably lead to a diminished need for government services through technological advances and increased competition from the private sector. This could result in a major change in the operation of government as Americans have known it.

Some knowledgeable people have predicted changes in the American form of government because of public labor disputes. These changes seem to be occurring in two directions, as pointed out by Arvid Anderson, chairman of New York City's Office of Collective Bargaining, in a statement to the 1970 annual proceedings of the United States Conference of Mayors.

> Collective bargaining in the public service is changing the Establishment in government at all levels. The impact on the structure of our government will be as profound, in my view, as the one-man-one-vote and civil rights decisions of the United States Supreme Court.
>
> One effect could be to speed the consolidation of local governmental units. Another effect has been the co-determination of conditions of employment.
>
> In time, collective bargaining will have as significant an effect on governmental institutions as it has had on political and economic institutions in the private sector.

One of the changes Anderson foresees will be a result of the attempts of government employees to make policy matters an issue of collective bargaining. As Anderson put it:

> The impact of collective bargaining on our society is also evidenced by the fact that a number of public employee organizations look upon it as a means for effectuating social change, as well as a procedure for improving wages, hours and fringe benefits. I refer to:

Teachers who want to bargain about the school curriculum or class size.

Welfare workers who want to bargain about the level of benefits of welfare recipients.

Interns who want to bargain about the quality of medical services offered.

Nurses who wish to bargain about the number of duty stations.

Policemen who want to regulate the number of men on a patrol or their authority to make arrests.

Air controllers who demand the right to bargain about their equipment and workloads.

Clearly, if these do become bargainable issues, then the traditional process of decision-making in government will be altered. Public officials will no longer be able to make policy decisions by fiat and leave it for the public and employees to accept them. School, police, hospital, welfare, and other types of officials at least will have to consult with employees, if not have the policies determined in collective bargaining.

This situation can be viewed as either beneficial or detrimental. On the one hand, it could lead to a broader decision-making process and a more democratic form of government. On the other hand, it could lead to a usurpation by the employees of authority traditionally invested in the people and their elected representatives. Anderson's view:

> While I consider all such [policy] topics as proper subjects of discussion between the public employer and employee organization, I do not agree that the collective bargaining process is the appropriate means of resolving all major public policy questions. In some

jurisdictions there are laws and procedures for resolving disputes over the scope of bargaining. In others *ad hoc* decisions are made.

The other effect collective bargaining could have on government would be to reduce the "balkanization" of local government. Most American cities are governed by a maze of rival, independent cities, counties, townships, school districts, and other special units. Metropolitan New York City, in a recent year, consisted of 1,476 governmental units, including three states (New York, New Jersey, and Connecticut), 555 incorporated towns and cities, and an almost inconceivable hodgepodge of counties, school districts, sewer and water districts, bridge, tunnel, highway, parking, and port authorities—to name a few.

Within the United States there are tens of thousands of governmental units. For a labor union to negotiate with all these units is extremely difficult. Jerry Wurf, president of the American Federation of State, County, and Municipal Employees, is among those advocating consolidation of the bargaining process.

> We have this crazy business of separate negotiations in literally hundreds of jurisdictions, which have so much in common. It leads to waste, upmanship, competition and all kinds of practices that are bad for both union and management. . . . I think [multi-unit bargaining] could be carried to the point that we could persuade various jurisdictions to set up similar job titles and job specifications and simplify the bargaining process and the whole personnel process. . . . Instead of dealing with 50 employers, we could deal with one, or perhaps four different groups of employers. . . . Sometimes you deal with 20 or 30

school boards in a relatively small geographic area. The economic dynamics are the same, the cost of living is the same, the labor market is the same, the job descriptions are the same. Well, isn't it kind of nutty to deal with 20, 30, 40 bosses when you can deal with one broad-based boss?

Political scientists have long decried the fragmentation of American local government. Indeed, America's urban problems are rooted in large measure in the multiplicity of governing units and the lack of leadership that results. Anderson, Wurf, and others see public sector collective bargaining as forcing some measure of unification on American local government.

Thus, as strikes, work stoppages, and labor disputes occur against governments in the United States, we are facing a problem with long-range implications on our form of government, as well as the immediate difficulties of interrupted governmental services and higher taxes. It is a relatively new problem, one for which no immediate solution is at hand. It is a problem likely to grow in the future. Above all, it is a problem that the readers of this book will be asked to help solve. I hope you will try.

Index

AFL-CIO. *See* American Federation of Labor–Congress of Industrial Organizations
AFSCME. *See* American Federation of State, County, and Municipal Employees
Abner, Willoughby, 78, 79, 136–137
Adams, John, 21
Adams, John Quincy, 21
Advisory Commission on Intergovernmental Relations, 93
Air controllers, 9, 128, 143
Alioto, Joseph, 70–71
American Arbitration Association, 136
American Federation of Labor–Congress of Industrial Organizations, 7, 78, 89, 90, 93, 95–96, 116, 123, 131
American Federation of State, County, and Municipal Employees, 7, 53, 54, 75–76, 77, 79, 93–94, 113, 144
American Federation of Teachers, 49, 53, 88
Anderson, Arvid, 134, 135, 142–143, 145
Arbitration, 108, 110, 127–128, 134, 135–136

Arthur, Chester A., 25
Association of Manufacturers, 120

Baird, James, 84
Baltimore, Maryland
  Police Department, 46
Banks, 15, 40
Binding arbitration. *See* Arbitration
Blount, Winton M., 57, 58, 59, 139
Boston, Massachusetts
  police strike, 31
Boycott, secondary, 106
Brooklyn *Eagle,* 113

Carnegie, Andrew, 29
Cavanagh, Jerome, 68
Cincinnati, Ohio
  sewage workers' strike, 10
Cities
  need for services, 9–10, 13, 140–141
Civil Service
  cause of labor unrest, 32, 39
  classification system, 32–33, 35
  examinations, 24, 26
  General Schedule, 32–33
  merit system, 25, 26
  personnel policy, 27
  promotions, 33, 35

INDEX

Civil Service, *Continued*
  reform, 20, 24–25, 29
  salaries, 24, 26, 27–28, 32–33, 35, 36, 44, 45, 60, 66
  transfers, 28
  turnover, 18, 22
  See also Postal employees; Public employees; Spoils system
Civil Service Commission. *See* United States Civil Service Commission
Civil War, 24
Classification Act, 26
Clay, Henry, 22
Cleveland, Ohio
  strike by municipal employees, 75–79
Codding, George A., Jr., 138, 139–140
Cogen, Charles, 49
Collective bargaining, 110–111, 112, 118, 134, 136, 142–145
  impact of, 143
  limited, 126, 129–130, 132
Congress. *See* United States Congress
Coolidge, Calvin, 31, 96
Corporations. *See* Private corporations
Corruption, 23–24
Crook County, Oregon, 46

Defense Department, 42
De Lury, John J., 88
Depression, 26, 40, 45
Detroit, Michigan
  police job action, 67–70
  riot, 69
  unions, 121
Detroit Police Officers Association, 67

Eisenhower Administration, 59
Employee Associations, 7, 52–53, 54
Emrich, Richard, 69
Emrich Commission, 69
Engineers, 28
  unemployed, 42–43
England
  sewage workers' strike, 10

Federal Deposit Insurance, 40–41

Federal employees. *See* Civil Service
Federal Labor Relations Council, 126–127, 132
Federal Management Improvement Conference, 117
Federal Mediation and Conciliation Service, 108, 118, 127
Federal Reserve Agency, 136–137
Federal Reserve system, 40
Federal Salary Reform Act, 27
Federal Service Impasses Panel, 127, 133
Ferguson Act, 84
Firemen, 5, 10, 36, 44, 113–114, 140
  "sick-out," 6
  "slowdown," 9
Foreign Service, 26
Fraternal Order of Police, 52

Garfield, James A., 25
General Motors, 111, 114, 141
Gildea, Jim, 131
Government employees. *See* Civil Service
Government regulation, 41
Government spending, 17
Graft. *See* Corruption
Grant, Ulysses S., 24
Grievance procedure, 108, 110, 118
Guiteau, Charles J., 25

Hampton, Robert E., 124–125, 128–129
Harrison, Benjamin, 25
Hayes, Rutherford B., 24–25
Highway workers, 13
  strike, 5, 6, 89–90
Hoover, Herbert, 26

Income, median family, 43–44
Industry. *See* Private corporations
Inflation, 80
Ingrassia, Tony, 129, 130
International Association of Fire Fighters, 52–53, 54
International City Management Association, 7

Jackson, Andrew, 21, 22
Jefferson, Thomas, 21, 22

147

INDEX

"Job actions," 9
   "rule book," 9
   "sick-out," 6, 9, 128, 168
   slowdown, 9
   "ticket slowdown," 68
Job security, 39–40, 41–43
Johnson, Lyndon B., 57, 126

Kappel, Frederick, 57
Kappel Commission, 57–58
Kennedy, John F., 27, 54, 126
King, Clarence, 75–76, 77, 78, 79
King, Martin Luther, Jr., 90
Kothe, Charles, 120

Labor-Management Relations Service, 5, 119
Labor relations
   inexperienced government officials, 116–117, 118–121
   power of management in government negotiations, 127, 132, 133
   See also Arbitration; Collective bargaining; Strikes; Unions
Labor unrest
   cause, 32, 39, 44, 47
   See also Strikes
Lincoln, Abraham, 23, 29
Lindsay, John V., 18–19
"Lockout," 106, 108

Madison, James, 21
Marcy, William Learned, 22
Mediators, 108, 110, 119
Mexican War, 24
Moffett, Kenneth, 118, 119
Monroe, James, 21
Moore, Arch, 89
Municipal employees
   labor relations, 134
   salaries, 45–46, 70–71, 74
   strikes, 5–6, 70–71, 74, 75–79
   See also Public employees

NALC. *See* National Association of Letter Carriers
NEA. *See* National Education Association
National Aeronautics and Space Agency, 42

National Association of Letter Carriers, 59, 63, 65, 85, 86
National Education Association, 53
National Labor Relations Board, 105, 127
National Postal Union, 132
New Deal, 27, 40, 41
New York City
   Board of Police Commissioners, 26
   governmental units, 144
   Office of Collective Bargaining, 134–135, 142
   police, 36
   Port of New York, 24
   public employees, 134–135
   salaries, 36
   strikes, 3, 18–19, 49, 55
   unions, 121
Nixon, Richard M., 18, 46, 58, 60, 62, 65, 126, 130, 132
Nurses, 140, 143

O'Brien, Larry, 57

Pendleton, George H., 25
Penn Central Railroad, 141
Pension benefits, 46
Police, 9–10, 36, 44, 113–114, 140, 143
   corruption, 26
   crime deterrent, 9
   salaries, 46, 67–68, 69–70
   strikes, 6, 31, 66–70
Politics, 114, 116
Postal Corporation, 60, 62
Postal employees, 33, 35
   salaries, 60, 66
   strike, 3, 15–16, 57–63, 65–66, 123–124, 128, 131, 132
   working conditions, 57–58
Postal system, 138–140
Post Office Department, 57, 60
Power failure, 13
Private corporations, 98, 100, 101, 102
   labor relations, 111, 113, 116
   profits, 102, 125
   stockholders, 98, 100, 125
Private industry. *See* Private corporations
Promotions, 33, 35, 36

INDEX

Public employees
  blue-collar workers, 53
  image, 29, 31
  inspectors, 17
  "job actions," 9
  numbers, 16
  strikes, 5–6
  See also Civil Service; Firemen; Municipal employees; Police; Postal employees; Teachers
Public transit, 10

Rademacher, James H., 59, 60, 61, 62–63, 65, 66, 84–85, 86, 89
Railroad industry, 141
Recession, 41
Retirement Act, 26
Riot, 69
Roche, James, 114
Rockefeller, John D., 29
Roosevelt, Franklin D., 26–27, 40
Roosevelt, Theodore, 25–26

St. Louis, Missouri, 46
Salaries, 24, 26, 27–28, 32–33, 35, 36, 37, 44–46, 60, 66, 67–68, 69–71, 74, 116, 130, 131–132
San Francisco, California
  municipal employees' strike, 70–71, 74
Sanitation men, 5, 6, 10, 140
Scarsdale, New York, 46–47
Schurz, Carl, 24–25
Scientists, 28
  unemployed, 42–43
Security and Exchange Commission, 41
Selden, David, 49, 88
Service Employees International Union, 53
Sewage workers
  strike, 10
Shanker, Albert, 88
Shultz, George P., 65
Silvergleid, David, 132–133
Social security, 40, 42
Social Security Administration, 35
Spivey, C. T., 117–118
Spoils system, 20–27
Stock exchanges, 15, 41
Stokes, Carl, 74–75, 76, 77–78, 79
Strikes, 5–6
  cause of, 112

Strikes, *Continued*
  effects of, 15–16, 19, 50, 80
  highway workers', 5, 6, 89–90
  laws, 31, 52, 55, 70, 75, 80, 82, 84, 85–86, 88, 89, 90, 92–93, 105, 112, 125
  municipal employees', 5–6, 70–71, 74, 75–79
  penalties, 82, 84–85, 88, 89
  police, 6, 31, 66–70
  postal employees', 3, 15–16, 57–63, 65–66, 123–124, 128, 131, 132
  racial overtones, 77–78
  right to strike, 106, 112, 113–114, 125
  sanitation men's, 5, 6
  sewage workers', 10
  sitdown strike, 106
  teachers', 6, 13, 15, 39, 49
  threatened, 7
  threat to health and safety, 3, 106
  transit employees', 10, 13, 18–19
  welfare workers', 6
  wildcat, 63, 110
  See also "Job actions"
Swarthout, Samuel, 24

Task Force on Employee-Management Relations, 126
Taxation, 17, 46–47, 52, 80, 102, 103
Taxpayers, 46–47, 70–71
Teachers, 140, 143
  advancement of, 37
  salaries of, 37
  strikes, 6, 13, 15, 39, 49
  unemployed, 43
Teamsters, 7, 75–76
Transfers, 28, 36
Transit employees, 9
  strikes, 10, 13, 18–19
Twentieth Century Fund, Task Force on Labor Disputes in Public Employment, 93

Unemployment, 42–43
Unions, 7, 53–55
  agency shop, 128
  checkoff, 84, 85
  contract, 108, 118
  elections, 105, 127

INDEX

Unions, *Continued*
   fragmentation of bargaining units, 121, 144–145
   government recognition, 126, 127, 136
   grievance procedures, 108, 110, 118
   membership, 7, 54
   no-strike pledge, 54, 60, 108
   officers, 105–106
   union shop, 128
   See also Arbitration; Collective bargaining; Strikes
United Auto Workers, 7
United Federation of Teachers, 88
United Mine Workers, 90, 141
United States Civil Service Commission, 25, 27, 28, 124, 129, 130
United States Conference of Mayors, 142
United States Congress
   Post Office Committees, 61–62
   salary decisions, 116, 130, 131–132
United States Steel Corporation, 117–118
Usery, W. J., Jr., 123, 131, 133–134

Van Buren, Martin, 22, 24
Voters, influence of, 121–122

Wages. *See* Salaries
Washington, George, 20–21, 22
Welfare workers, 143
   strike, 6
West Virginia
   road employees' strike in, 89–90
Wirtz, Willard, 126
Work stoppages. *See* Strikes
Wurf, Jerry, 77, 78, 79, 113, 114, 126, 144–145

Youngstown, Ohio, 47

Zagoria, Sam, 119–120